Guinea:

Malaria Operational Plan FY 2014

TABLE OF CONTENTS

TABLE OF CONTENTS..2

ABBREVIATIONS AND ACRONYMS..3

EXECUTIVE SUMMARY..4

STRATEGY...8

    INTRODUCTION..8

    MALARIA SITUATION IN GUINEA...9

    COUNTRY HEALTH SYSTEM DELIVERY STRUCTURE AND MOH ORGANIZATION......................10

    COUNTRY MALARIA CONTROL STRATEGY..11

    INTEGRATION, COLLABORATION AND COORDINATION...................................12

    PMI GOALS, TARGETS & INDICATORS...12

    PROGRESS ON COVERAGE/IMPACT INDICATORS TO DATE.............................13

    OTHER RELEVANT EVIDENCE ON PROGRESS..15

    CHALLENGES, OPPORTUNITIES & THREATS...15

        Challenges and threats..15

        Opportunities..16

    PMI SUPPORT STRATEGY...16

OPERATIONAL PLAN..18

    PREVENTION...18

        Insecticide-Treated Nets...18

        Indoor Residual Spraying...20

        Malaria in Pregnancy...21

    CASE MANAGEMENT...25

        Diagnosis...25

        Treatment..28

        Pharmaceutical Management..32

    MONITORING & EVALUATION AND OPERATIONAL RESEARCH........................36

    BEHAVIOR CHANGE COMMUNICATION..42

    HEALTH SYSTEM STRENGTHENING AND CAPACITY BUILDING.......................44

    STAFFING & ADMINISTRATION..47

TABLE 1..49

TABLE 2..50

ABBREVIATIONS AND ACRONYMS

AS-AQ	Artesunate-amodiaquine
ACTs	Artemisinin-based Combination Therapy
ANC	Antenatal care
BCC	Behavior change communication
CDC	Centers for Disease Control and Prevention
CHWs	Community health workers
DHS	Demographic Health Survey
DNPL	National Directorate of Pharmacies and Laboratory
EPI	Expanded program on immunization
EU	European Union
EUV	End-use verification
FY	Fiscal year
Global Fund	Global Fund to Fight AIDS, Tuberculosis and Malaria
GOG	Government of Guinea
HMIS	Health Management Information System
IDB	Islamic Development Bank
IRS	Indoor residual spray
IPTp	Intermittent preventive treatment for pregnant women
ITN	Insecticide-treated nets
LLIN	Long lasting insecticide-treated net
M&E	Monitoring and evaluation
MIP	Malaria in pregnancy
MIS	Malaria Indicator Survey
MOH	Ministry of Health and Public Hygiene
NMCP	National Malaria Control Program
NGO	Non-governmental organization
PCG	Central Pharmacy of Guinea
PMI	President's Malaria Initiative
RBM	Roll Back Malaria
RDT	Rapid Diagnostic Test
SP	Sulphadoxine-pyrimethamine
USAID	United States Agency for International Development
UNICEF	United Nations Children's Fund
WHO	World Health Organization

EXECUTIVE SUMMARY

Malaria prevention and control are major foreign assistance objectives of the U.S. Government. In May 2009, President Barack Obama announced the Global Health Initiative (GHI) to reduce the burden of disease and promote healthy communities and families around the world. The President's Malaria Initiative (PMI) is a core component of the GHI, along with Human immunodeficiency virus/acquired immunodeficiency syndrome, tuberculosis, maternal and child health, family planning and reproductive health, nutrition, and neglected tropical diseases.

PMI was launched in June 2005 as a five-year, $1.2 billion initiative to rapidly scale up malaria prevention and treatment interventions and reduce malaria-related mortality by 50% in 15 high-burden countries in sub-Saharan Africa. With the passage of the 2008 Lantos-Hyde Act, funding was extended and, as part of the GHI, the goal of PMI was adjusted to reduce malaria-related mortality by 70% in the original 15 countries by the end of 2015. Programming of PMI activities follows the core principles of GHI: encouraging country ownership and investing in country-led plans and health systems; increasing impact and efficiency through strategic coordination and programmatic integration; strengthening and leveraging key partnerships, multilateral organizations, and private contributions; implementing a woman- and girl-centered approach; improving monitoring and evaluation (M&E); and promoting research and innovation.

In June 2011, Guinea was selected to receive funding during the sixth year of PMI. Guinea has year-round malaria transmission with high transmission from July through October in most areas. Malaria is considered the number one public health problem in the country. National statistics in Guinea show that among children less than five years of age, malaria accounts for 31% of consultations, 25% of hospitalizations, and 14% of hospital deaths in public facilities.

A Demographic and Health Survey (DHS) was carried out in mid-2012, and the results provide concrete baseline information for key malaria indicators. The DHS reported a wide range of malaria prevalence across Guinea's regions, ranging from 66% in Faranah to 3% in Conakry, but with a relatively high prevalence of 44% as the national average. Survey estimates show that approximately 47% of households own at least one insecticide-treated net (ITN), and 26% and 28% of children under five and pregnant women, respectively, slept under an ITN the night before the survey. Roughly 18% of women surveyed had received at least two doses of intermittent preventive treatment during their last pregnancy, and less than 1% of children under five with fever in the two weeks preceding the survey received artemisinin-based combination therapy (ACT) on the same or next day of fever development.

This FY 2014 Malaria Operational Plan (MOP) was developed with the participation of the National Malaria Control Program (NMCP) and other country partners during a planning visit carried out on June 17-27, 2013by staff from the U.S. Agency for International Development (USAID) and the Centers for Disease Control and Prevention (CDC).The activities that PMI is proposing for this Year 4 complement the contributions of other partners and directly support the NMCP's new strategic plan. PMI will support select activities related to malaria policies and health system strengthening on a nation-wide level, with remaining activities targeted to Conakry's five communes and 14 of Guinea's prefectures. Global Fund to Fight AIDS, Tuberculosis and Malaria (Global Fund) efforts will target the remaining 19 prefectures of the country (after a period of suspension, the Global Fund has consolidated its Round 6 and 10 grants with an international non-governmental organization (NGO) as the principal recipient and the NMCP as sub-recipient). The proposed FY 2014 PMI budget for Guinea is $10 million. The following paragraphs describe current progress to date as well as the FY 2014 plans:

Insecticide-Treated Nets (ITNs): The new national malaria strategy is to support free distribution of long-lasting insecticide-treated nets (LLINs) through antenatal care (ANC) and vaccination clinics; free distribution through mass campaigns; and the sale of LLINs in the commercial sector. Guinea has started a nationwide, universal coverage campaign. In May 2013, more than 3.2 million LLINs were distributed in the 19 prefectures supported by the Global Fund. The campaign will be completed in the remaining 14 prefectures and five communes of Conakry in September/October 2013 with 1,590,000 bed nets procured by PMI and 1 million nets funded by the Islamic Development Bank (IDB) through United Nations Children's Fund (UNICEF); operations and distribution costs will be supported by PMI with FY 2013 resources. With FY 2014 funding, PMI will procure 180,000 LLINs for distribution in health facilities during ANC services in PMI target prefectures. In addition, PMI plans to support behavior change communication (BCC) activities, including mass media and community-level approaches (e.g., local radio stations, women's groups) to increase demand for and promote correct and consistent use of LLINs.

Indoor Residual Spraying (IRS): The new national malaria strategy includes IRS. Limited spraying in the country is carried out by mining companies which spray the homes of their workers in villages surrounding their compounds. Current PMI support is being used to conduct standard entomological surveillance including species identification and insecticide resistance, and to build capacity of key personnel to conduct and manage an entomological surveillance program. With FY 2014 funds, PMI will continue to support surveillance and support skills building within the NMCP and other national structures to conduct entomologic surveillance.

Malaria in Pregnancy (MIP): In 2013, the NMCP will finalize revisions of its national strategy and adopt current World Health Organization (WHO) recommendations for intermittent preventive treatment of pregnant women (IPTp) with sulphadoxine-pyrimethamine (SP) at each ANC visit and LLIN distribution at the first ANC visit. The revised strategy will base its annual SP needs on three treatments per pregnancy. PMI will work with the NMCP to ensure that the national strategy updates annual pregnancy estimations, which are currently based on percentage of women of reproductive age rather than actual pregnancy rates. During the past year, preliminary 2012 DHS results were released, which showed that although 85% of pregnant women make at least one ANC visit, only 18% received at least 2 doses of IPTp. No LLINs were available for routine distribution anywhere in Guinea. PMI, in an effort to stem the SP stockout crisis, which may be a contributing factor to the low SP coverage indicated in the DHS results, delivered 375,000 treatments in December 2012. PMI also trained 419 health workers and 206 community agents and reached over 168,000 people with information on prevention of MIP. With FY 2014 funding, PMI will procure 1,437,500 treatments of SP and 180,000 LLINs, as well as continue support for training, supervision, and awareness-raising around the importance of MIP.

Case Management – Diagnosis: The current national policy is to confirm suspect malaria cases with a Rapid Diagnostic Test (RDT) or microscopy before prescribing a treatment of ACT, both at the facility and community levels. The policy also recommends that each health facility have a microscope for diagnostic confirmation of cases, although in practice, microscopes are only available in hospitals and some health centers. PMI has begun to assist with the scale up of malaria diagnostics by training health workers in use of both RDTs and microscopy. In FY 2011 and FY 2012, 100,000 and 1 million RDTs, respectively, were procured to start progressive health facility- and community-level training to address the country's diagnostic needs. Additionally, PMI has ordered microscopes and reagents to be delivered to referral hospitals throughout the country. The PMI partner has also provided technical assistance in microscopy by building in-country laboratory capacity. With FY 2014 funding, PMI will procure approximately 4,515,000 RDTs to continue scaling up RDT use in health facilities and in communities via community health workers (CHWs) in PMI target areas, and will continue to support malaria microscopy by procuring 15 microscopes, reagents, slides and repair materials for hospitals. PMI also plans to support training of laboratory technicians at hospitals and health centers and help reinforce quality assurance and quality control for microscopy by working with the National Laboratory and the NMCP, while continuing training of health workers and CHWs in proper RDT use.

Case Management - Treatment: In Guinea, artesunate-amodiaquine (AS-AQ) is the recommended treatment for uncomplicated malaria cases, while injectable artesunate has just been adopted for treatment of severe malaria. Although ACTs procured by PMI in late 2011 and 2012 have helped to fill a large nationwide gap, the concern remains that, eventually, this supply might run out and the country will face stockouts once again. However, some progress has been made in resolving Global Fund issues and releasing funds, and important stock of ACTs was ordered for the country. In addition to ACT procurement, PMI supported the training of health personnel in malaria case management, as well as supervision of health personnel to improve the quality of treatment in PMI target areas. With FY 2014 funding, PMI will procure and distribute approximately 1,833,000 ACTs for treatment of uncomplicated malaria, and 71,300 treatments of injectable artesunate for treatment of severe malaria. PMI also plans to support training and supervision of health workers and CHWs and support the scale up of community case management in PMI target areas.

Pharmaceutical Management: The national policy is to deliver malaria treatment and prevention commodities through the public system via the *Pharmacie Centrale de Guinée* (PCG). In 2011 and 2012, PMI supported a round table discussion to bring all partners together and begin work on restoring the capacity of PCG and the public sector delivery system to function as intended. As a result, PMI has put in place a comprehensive package of technical assistance to strengthen the supply chain and the pharmaceutical system and create conditions for drug distribution, although some resistance to improving the governance of PCG has become evident. With FY 2014 funding, PMI will continue to support technical assistance to improve the public pharmaceutical system, and in collaboration with the European Union (EU) and other partners, work to resolve the outstanding issues. Support from PMI will contribute to strengthening the national supply chain as a whole and result in a greatly improved Guinean health sector.

Monitoring and Evaluation (M&E): While the national strategy is near finalization, the NMCP, with PMI support, is still working to develop its revised national M&E plan, including a costing plan. The 2012 DHS, including malaria parasitemia estimates, will serve as a baseline for PMI and the country itself, as it works to achieve Roll Back Malaria (RBM) objectives by 2015. PMI will also support a Malaria Indicator Survey (MIS) in 2014, which will provide meaningful interim estimates for malaria indicators, particularly LLIN coverage and use following the universal coverage distribution campaign. With FY 2014 funding, PMI will support an end-use verification (EUV) survey. Under the malaria bilateral project, PMI will continue to provide M&E training at regional and district levels and support health facility-based surveillance to monitor longitudinal trends in select facilities. PMI will also provide technical assistance for M&E to help strengthen the national health information system.

Behavior Change Communication (BCC): The NMCP and partners revised its national malaria communication plan in March 2012. The plan emphasizes appropriate strategies and channels to reach various target groups with culturally sound information on malaria prevention and control. PMI has supported this process and will continue to work to ensure that there is national consensus as well as key partner input in the design of activities and that uniform indicators and targets are used to monitor progress and assess the impact of BCC activities throughout the country. In FY 2014, in accordance with PMI BCC guidance and under the malaria bilateral project, BCC will be part of an integrated communications package including ITN use, MIP, and community case management. This activity will be implemented in health districts targeted by PMI, using the NMCP communication plan.

Health Systems Strengthening/Capacity Building: Given the challenges facing malaria prevention and control in Guinea, PMI resources will focus on addressing priorities that are directly linked to malaria service delivery. PMI will continue to work with other donors to build in-country capacity in various technical areas in malaria prevention and control. PMI will support improvement of coordination among key stakeholders to enable the NMCP to fill the service gap, making maximum use of current and potential resources provided by partners. With FY 2014 funds, PMI will support entomology training of NMCP personnel, assist in training of NMCP staff in management and M&E, and provide support to the NMCP to conduct supervision and maintain basic office operations including communication with other partners and stakeholders. This effort will be documented to serve as a best practice in institutional capacity building to inform mission initiatives to build capacity in select institutions within the health sector.

STRATEGY

Introduction

The President's Malaria Initiative (PMI) was launched in June 2006 as a five-year, $1.2 billion initiative to rapidly scale up malaria prevention and treatment interventions and reduce malaria-related mortality in 15 high-burden countries in sub-Saharan Africa. With the passage of the 2008 Lantos-Hyde Act, funding was extended and, as part of the GHI, the goal of PMI was adjusted to reduce malaria-related mortality by 70% in the original 15 countries by the end of 2015. This goal will be achieved by continuing to scale up coverage of the most vulnerable groups – children under five years of age and pregnant women – with proven preventive and therapeutic interventions, including artemisinin-based combination therapies (ACTs), insecticide-treated nets (ITNs), intermittent preventive treatment for pregnant women (IPTp), and indoor residual spraying (IRS).

Guinea was one of four additional countries selected for PMI focus in 2011. Since program launch PMI has supported the following: two emergency procurements of ACTs to respond to nationwide stockouts, as well as one procurement to maintain existing supplies throughout the country; activities to improve the poorly functioning pharmaceutical sector; training and supervision exercises to improve quality of malaria services being delivered at both facility and community levels; procurement of commodities including ITNs for a nationwide campaign, sulphadoxine-pyrimethamine (SP) for pregnant women, and rapid diagnostic tests (RDTs); and behavior change communications (BCC). PMI will continue to build on these efforts moving forward into Year 4.

Global Fund to Fight AIDS, Tuberculosis and Malaria (Global Fund) resources for Guinea for both Round 6 and 10 were consolidated into one grant in 2012, and funds have been disbursed to support key activities, such as those related to the 2013 nationwide net campaign. As part of the consolidation process, the National Malaria Control Program (NMCP) was removed as a principal recipient, with all funds now being passed through Catholic Relief Services as the PR; the NMCP will remain as a sub-recipient. In the past year, other partners have come forward to support Guinea's national malaria strategy, including the Islamic Development Bank (IDB) and the Government of Japan, who purchased 1 million and 290,000 long-lasting insecticidal nets (LLINs), respectively, as contributions to the nationwide campaign. With support from PMI and Global Fund, the NMCP hopes to cover much of the country's remaining needs in commodities, technical assistance, and capacity building, but additional resources will be required for the country to start IRS activities in areas beyond where private mining companies currently operate. PMI is supporting the NMCP to take a greater lead in coordination and organizing meetings with major stakeholders to ensure that nationwide coverage targets are achieved.

This FY 2014 Malaria Operational Plan (MOP) presents a detailed plan for the fourth year of PMI in Guinea, based on the PMI guidance and the NMCP's five-year National Malaria Control Strategy (2013-2017). The MOP was developed in consultation with the NMCP and with the participation of many national and international partners involved with malaria prevention and control in the country. All proposed activities were reviewed and endorsed by partners, including the Ministry of Health and Public Hygiene (MOH), at a stakeholders meeting held at the end of the planning visit. This document reviews the current status of malaria control policies and interventions in Guinea, describes progress to date, identifies challenges and unmet needs if the targets of the NMCP and PMI are to be achieved, and provides a description of planned FY 2014 activities.

Malaria Situation in Guinea

Guinea is a coastal country in West Africa composed of four areas with distinct ecologies: Lower Guinea, which includes the coastal lowlands; Middle Guinea, the mountainous region running north-south in the middle of the country; the Sahelian Upper Guinea; and the forested jungle area in the south. Guinea borders Guinea-Bissau and Senegal to the north, Mali and Côte d'Ivoire to the east, and Liberia and Sierra Leone to the south. Guinea's 33 prefectures (or districts) are grouped into eight administrative regions, one of which is the capital city of Conakry and its five communes. Guinea's entire population of 10.8 million people is at risk of malaria.[1,2] According to the 2011 Human Development Index, Guinea has among the lowest health and development indicators, ranking 178 out of 187 countries.[3] Poverty has been steadily increasing over the past decade, and as of 2010 over half (58%) of Guinea's population lives below the Guinean government's poverty line of $196 USD per person per year.[4] Infant and under-five mortality rates are 81 and 130 per 1,000 live births, respectively.[5] Although the antenatal care (ANC) coverage of at least 1 visit is high (88%), the lifetime risk of maternal death is one of the worst in the world, at 1 in 26.[6]

Guinea has year-round malaria transmission with peak transmission from July through October in most areas.[7] According to the National Malaria Control Strategy, malaria remains the number one public health problem in Guinea, with 98% of malaria infections caused by *Plasmodium falciparum*. According to national health statistics, the morbidity rate for malaria is 148/1,000 population. National statistics in Guinea show that among children less than five years of age, malaria accounts for 31% of consultations, 25% of hospitalizations, and 14% of hospital deaths.[8] This estimate does not include malaria cases seen in the community or in private facilities. Among the general population, malaria is also the primary cause of consultations (34%), hospitalizations (31%), and death (14%) according to the MOH.[9]Most malaria cases reported in national statistics are clinically diagnosed, and therefore may not accurately reflect the true malaria burden.

According to the preliminary results of the 2012 Demographic and Health Survey (DHS), the prevalence of malaria ranges between 3.3% (in Conakry) and 66.3% (in Faranah) with a national prevalence of 43.9% for children 6-59 months using microscopy (47% based on RDT results).

[1]https://www.cia.gov/library/publications/the-world-factbook/geos/gv.html
[2] According the NMCP 2013 gap analysis, the population in 2014 is projected to be 11,767,987.
[3]UNDP 2011 Human Development Report. Available at: http://hdr.undp.org/en/reports/global/hdr2011/download/
[4] International Monetary Fund: Guinea: Poverty Reduction Strategy Paper - Annual Progress Report: http://www.imf.org/external/pubs/ft/scr/2012/cr1261.pdf.
[5]UNICEF: The State of the World's Children 2012. Available at: http://www.unicef.org/sowc2012/statistics.php.
[6]UNICEF: The State of the World's Children 2012. Available at: http://www.unicef.org/sowc2012/statistics.php.
[7] National Malaria Control Strategy 2006-2010.
[8] Malaria M&E Strategy 2008-2012.
[9] Plan de Gestion des Achats et des Stocks, May 2011.

Parasitemia prevalence shows strong variations by place of residence with 53% in rural areas compared to 18% in urban areas (strongly influenced by Conakry).

Coverage estimates for key interventions show room for improvement in reaching targets. A little more than half of households surveyed have at least one mosquito net, treated or untreated (53%), while 47% of households own at least 1 ITN. These proportions are somewhat higher in rural areas (55% and 50%) than in urban (48% and 42%). The proportions of children who slept under any mosquito net and under an ITN the night before the survey are 29% and 26%, respectively. These proportions are higher in rural areas (30% and 27%) than in urban (28% and 24%). In households with an ITN, the proportion of children under 5 years who slept under an ITN the night before the survey was 51% with no difference between urban and rural households. One in three pregnant women reported sleeping under any mosquito net (33%) while 28% reported sleeping under an ITN. In households with an ITN, the proportion of pregnant women who slept under an ITN the night before the survey was 59%. This proportion is higher in urban (62%) than rural (58%) areas. Coverage with IRS remains relatively low due to limited IRS activities in the country. Among children less than 5 years old with fever in the 2 weeks before the survey, only 0.5% received an ACT on the same or next day. While 17% received any antimalarial treatment (same or next day), the majority of these (6.1%) received chloroquine.

Country Health System Delivery Structure and MOH Organization

The health care system in Guinea is managed by the MOH and based on the administrative division of the country into eight regions. Within the 8 regions are 38 health districts composed of 334 rural communities and 38 urban municipalities. The MOH has three levels in its administrative structure: central, intermediate, and peripheral.

Public health facilities are organized into three levels that provide primary, secondary and tertiary health care:
1. The first level is represented by the health district and consists of three levels:[10]
   - About 963 health posts provide basic primary care and serve several villages (about 3,000 people) each. Health posts are staffed by an *Agent Technique de Santé*, a clinical officer with three years of training.
   - About 413 health centers provide preventive and curative care and supervise the health posts. Health centers are staffed by several clinicians, including nurses, midwives and doctors.
   - About 33 district hospitals serve as a reference for health centers and provide care to an average of 285,777 people in the district. .
2. The second level is represented by the regional hospital and serves as a reference for the districts. There are 7 regional hospitals plus 9 municipal hospitals providing care to an estimated 1,401,400 people in the region.
3. The third level consists of the university hospitals at the national level. This is the highest level of reference for specialized care and includes two such hospitals in the country.

---

[10] The number of health posts and hospitals are based on 2011 estimates; the number of health centers is based on a 2013 estimate.

In addition to public structures, Guinea has a large number of private structures and traditional practitioners. At the community level, Health and Hygiene Committees are responsible for understanding health issues, monitoring health programs, and coordinating with local medical officers to improve access to and quality of care in their communities.

Access to care is a major problem in Guinea, and the MOH estimates that only around 55% of the population has access to public health care services. The MOH is investing heavily in community case management through a trained nationwide cadre of community health workers (CHWs) to expand health care access to communities, especially in remote and inaccessible areas. A comprehensive policy on community health care has been elaborated but not yet validated; more than 3,000 CHWs have been trained and now provide health education and basic curative care to surrounding communities. The cadre of CHWs has been specifically trained to diagnose malaria and provide ACTs to patients with uncomplicated malaria. Guinea's MOH strongly supports integration of priority national health programs, including malaria, HIV/AIDS, neglected tropical diseases, nutrition, reproductive health and family planning, safe delivery, and epidemic surveillance.

Country Malaria Control Strategy

The new National Malaria Control Strategic Plan, 2013-2017 was developed (but has not yet been validated) with the inputs of partners and stakeholders. The goal of the new strategy is to contribute to the reduction of malaria morbidity and mortality by scaling up universal access to effective preventive and treatment interventions. The specific objective is to reduce malaria morbidity by 75% compared to 2000 levels and to reduce malaria mortality to near zero by the end of 2017. The national strategy's goal, objective, and interventions will be in line with international guidelines put forth by Roll Back Malaria (RBM) and the World Health Organization (WHO), once the strategy and policy documents are revised.

The strategy is built on three components:
1. Prevention through: the use of LLINs, which are distributed free through mass distribution campaigns and routine distribution channels; uptake of IPTp; use of IRS; and collective measures to destroy larvae in identifiable and accessible breeding sites.
2. Treatment of uncomplicated cases with ACTs at health facilities and the community level, and treatment of severe cases with injectable artesunate, injectable artemether, or quinine. Laboratory confirmation by RDT or microscopy is required before treatment.
3. Cross-cutting support strategies including epidemiological and entomological surveillance; monitoring and evaluation (M&E); quality control of drugs and laboratory diagnostics; and BCC.

The NMCP has outlined some changes in the new 2013-2017 strategy including:
- The introduction of injectable artesunate for treatment of severe malaria cases in addition to injectable artemether or quinine; and
- A new policy for IPTp stating that a dose of SP should be given at each ANC visit, assuming visits are at least one month apart, after the first trimester.

The new strategy includes the following priorities in the fight against malaria:

- Mobilization of resources through the development of a coherent and realistic strategic plan accompanied by sufficient funding from the government, private sector, and international donors;
- Availability of sufficient quantities of commodities, including LLINs, RDTs, microscopy equipment, and treatments;
- Capacity building for diagnosis and case management in the public sector, private sector (including faith-based organizations), and at the community level;
- Capacity building of community actors and civil society, including non-governmental organizations (NGOs) and community-based organizations in the fight against malaria; and
- Capacity building for the NMCP for planning, coordination, and M&E.

Integration, Collaboration and Coordination

The goal of integration is to increase efficiency in the use of available health resources in the country and coordinate the participation of partners in order to reduce malaria mortality and morbidity among children and pregnant women. According to the new national strategy, dwindling resources, the involvement of various partners, and the need to rapidly scale up interventions highlight the necessity and urgency of developing mechanisms for integration and effective coordination at national, regional, and district levels.

Strengthening community participation in the planning and delivery of health services is a challenge requiring the active involvement of community networks, structured groups, and opinion leaders in all villages. Partnership between private and public entities is another challenge that will be achieved through a contractual approach in the implementation of control activities. Integration of the private and religious sectors in Guinea is a priority. In the five communes of Conakry, a substantial number of patients seek care at faith-based private health structures before public health facilities. Importantly, the MOH has established an intersector collaboration by developing a partnership between the MOH and other non-health sectors such as education, environment, social affairs, the private sector, and other non-governmental structures.

Malaria partners in Guinea include: WHO, World Bank, PMI, Japanese International Cooperation Agency, German Development Cooperation, IDB, United Nations Children's Fund (UNICEF), Global Fund, African Development Bank, *Medecins sans Frontières*, Population Services International, Engender Health, Catholic Relief Services, and other regional organizations

PMI Goals, Targets & Indicators

The goal of PMI is to reduce malaria-associated mortality by 70% compared to pre-Initiative levels in the 15 original PMI countries and to reduce malaria-associated mortality by 50% in new countries added to PMI in FY 2010 and later, including Guinea. By the end of 2014, PMI will assist Guinea to achieve the following targets in populations at risk for malaria:

- >90% of households with a pregnant woman and/or children under five will own at least one ITN;

- 85% of children under five will have slept under an ITN the previous night;
- 85% of pregnant women will have slept under an ITN the previous night;
- 85% of houses in geographic areas targeted for IRS will have been sprayed;
- 85% of pregnant women and children under five will have slept under an ITN the previous night or in a house that has been sprayed with IRS in the last 6 months;
- 85% of women who have completed a pregnancy in the last two years will have received two or more doses of IPTp during that pregnancy; and
- 85% of government health facilities have ACTs available for treatment of uncomplicated malaria; and
- 85% of children under five with suspected or confirmed malaria will have received treatment with ACTs within 24 hours of onset of their symptoms.

Progress on Coverage/Impact Indicators to Date

Progress in malaria prevention and treatment can be assessed by comparing the standardized coverage indicators for ITN ownership and use, IPTp, and prompt and effective treatment across national household surveys. The 2012 DHS provides the first national parasitemia measures. Important progress is shown between the 2005 and 2012 DHS, likely reflecting support from Global Fund Rounds 2 and 6, including a targeted ITN distribution campaign in 2009. In recent years, however, stockouts of bednets, ACTs, and other commodities have slowed initial gains, as reflected in the 2012 DHS results.

According to the 2005 DHS, only 27% of households owned any mosquito net with less than 4% owning a treated net (ITN). Only 1% of children under 5 and pregnant women reported sleeping under an ITN. Less than 3% of women reported receiving at least two doses of SP during their last pregnancy. The 2007 MICS showed slight improvements in ITN ownership and use, but these rates are still quite low.

The 2009 and 2010 national coverage surveys, conducted with Global Fund financing, appear to show substantial improvements in key indicators. After a nationwide targeted bednet distribution campaign in 2009, the 2010 survey predictably shows increases in ITN ownership and use: 79% of households reported owning at least 1 ITN, and 60% of children under five and 47% of pregnant women reported sleeping under an ITN, respectively. Even more striking are the apparent gains in IPTp coverage in 2009 and 2010 compared to the 2005 DHS. While not even 3% of women received 2 or more doses of SP during their last pregnancy in 2005, 36% and 41% received it in 2009 and 2010, respectively. Direct comparisons between the DHS and the 2009 and 2010 national coverage surveys should be made with caution due to some apparent methodological differences in how indicators were calculated and reported. The specific differences are noted in the indicator table.

The 2012 DHS provides an important data point for ITN coverage since it was conducted prior to the universal coverage campaign (which is currently ongoing). Not surprisingly, since over two years have passed since the last targeted distribution (with no routine distribution in the interim), ITN coverage and use indicators have dropped since the 2010 survey, with less than half of all households reportedly owning an ITN, and 26% and 28% of children under 5 and pregnant women, respectively, reporting sleeping under an ITN. Coverage of IPTp (2 doses of SP) has also dropped to 18%. The prompt and effective treatment indicator is particularly low with less than 1% of children under 5 with fever receiving treatment with ACTs within the same or next day of fever onset. Estimates for malaria-associated anemia (cut-off value <8g/dl) are not yet available from the preliminary 2012 DHS results, but the country's first parasitemia measures (via microscopy) show an estimated prevalence of 44% for the country. Conakry has the lowest prevalence at 3%, while the regions with the highest prevalence estimates are Faranah and N'Zérékoré with 66% and 59%, respectively. Neither Faranah nor N'Zérékoré are in the PMI target zones.

The table below summarizes coverage indicators for malaria control, as well as anemia and parasitemia, from national household surveys since 2005. Due to some variations in survey methodology, not all indicators are directly comparable; please consider the footnotes at the bottom of the table.

Malaria Indicator	DHS 2005	MICS 2007	National Coverage Surveys		DHS 2012 *Preliminary results*
			2009	2010	
Percent of households with at least one ITN	3.5%	12.5%	23.4%	78.8%	47.4%
Percent of children under five who slept under an ITN the previous night	1.4%	6.7%	12.0%	60.4%	26.1%
Percent of pregnant who slept under an ITN the previous night	1.4%	5.1%	24.7%*	46.8%*	28.3%
Percent of women who received 2+ doses of IPTp during their last pregnancy in the last 2 years	2.7%	-	35.9%**	41.0%**	17.8%
Percent of children under 5 with fever in the last 2 weeks who received treatment with ACTs within 24 hours of onset of fever	***	***	1.3%	***	0.5%
Percent of children under 5 with severe anemia (<8g/dl) *(Note: A cut-off value for <8g/dl, typically associated with malaria, was not available from the preliminary DHS2012 results)*	14.5%	-	-	-	Pending
Percent of children under 5 with parasitemia (microscopy/RDT)	-	-	-	-	43.9%

* The 2009 survey report specifies use of LLINs by pregnant women while the 2010 survey report does not (i.e., it includes any treated nets).
** The 2009 and 2010 coverage surveys include a five-year look-back period instead of a two-year period and do not specify that at least one dose was taken at an ANC visit.
*** ACTs were not the first-line treatment at the time of the DHS and MICS surveys; the 2010 coverage survey report did not provide adequate data to calculate this indicator in the standard format (i.e., the denominator could not be determined).

Other Relevant Evidence on Progress

As PMI begins its third year of program implementation and benefits from some continuity of operations, it is evident that the country's malaria program has achieved (or is in the process of achieving) some major milestones: the first universal coverage LLIN mass campaign, achieving a relatively continuous supply of ACTs, roll out of RDTs, and the first nationally representative parasitemia estimates. In addition to these milestones, there is also evidence of increased capacity at the NMCP to coordinate and guide activities throughout the country. New staff have been hired and important processes such as the Malaria Program Review have helped the program to take a critical look at its operations and revise its national strategy and policies. Important research on therapeutic efficacy, seasonal malaria burden, and community knowledge, attitudes and behaviors related to malaria are ongoing. PMI, together with its partners will continue to build on this momentum and contribute to meeting the NMCP's goal of reducing malaria morbidity and mortality in Guinea through universal access to malaria prevention and treatment.

Challenges, Opportunities & Threats

Challenges and threats

The NMCP infrastructure is weakened by inadequate material, human, and financial resources:
- Variable electricity supply, no generator, no network internet connectivity, little fuel for vehicles, and a difficult location in the middle of a busy market pose challenges to productivity.
- Staff with varying levels of expertise (and in some cases with unclear terms of reference) prevent the NMCP from performing at full potential given limited resources.
- Lack of finances precludes the NMCP from procuring needed supplies and commodities and meeting operational expenses. As an illustration, only 2.54% (approximately $22 million) of the national budget is allocated to the health sector by the Government of Guinea (GOG). Seventy percent of the annual national budget pays for salaries, leaving only $6 million to purchase vaccines and support management of health facilities.

Limitations to capacity for case management are linked to the following constraints:
- Limited commodities, including stockouts of LLINs, RDTs, ACTs, and SP, compromise service delivery to the most vulnerable populations, leaving universal access and coverage currently unachieved.
- Low use of IPTp and treatment seeking is complicated by minimal involvement and weak inter-sector coordination of key stakeholders, namely private and religious sectors, community opinion leaders, elected officials, and community-based organizations who could help improve social mobilization and BCC.
- A lack of health care providers and supervisors results in non-adherence to the national policy by providers.

Inadequate M&E and data collection systems (health and logistical information management) limit the NMCP's ability to obtain reliable data on disease burden, service access and utilization, quality and quantity of services provided, and needs, stocks and consumption of commodities to guide policy and practice.

15

In Guinea, the supply chain and pharmaceutical system is very weak, and attempts from PMI and other donors to assist with addressing major systemic weaknesses are challenged or slowed down by certain authorities. Also, the recurrent political unrest due to lack of clear dialogue between the ruling government and opposition about the legislative election represents a threat to smooth implementation of health interventions, mostly in Conakry, where PMI covers the five communes.

Opportunities

PMI and Global Fund represent good opportunities to make progress in malaria control in Guinea, although the delay in the start of Global Fund activities has had a negative impact on the NMCP and the population. The two institutions have recently improved their communication in order to anticipate issues about Guinea's funding from the Global Fund. Other partners such as WHO, UNICEF, the World Bank and a few local NGOs are considered good opportunities for leveraging resources, but they are not fully engaged with the NMCP. The strong potential for collaboration with the Peace Corps includes having volunteers support malaria prevention and education activities. Additionally, the development of the training and research center at Maferinyah has the potential to support improved training and research in Guinea.

Although considered symbolic, the contribution of mining companies to malaria control efforts in Guinea is an opportunity that can be better leveraged with stronger coordination and constant dialogue between the GOG and Mining Operators.

The GOG is taking some strides towards improving the performance of the health sector. A national health forum is slated to take place in late August 2013 with the aim of sharpening its health governance efforts and focusing on strengthening the health system (supply chain and pharmaceutical system management, transparency and accountability in the health sector, service delivery, and BCC).

PMI Support Strategy

In supporting Guinea's National Malaria Strategic Plan, PMI focuses on the key intervention areas of ITN use, IPTp, and case management, including support for malaria diagnostics and treatment at the health facility and community levels. PMI also supports the cross-cutting areas of commodity management, entomological monitoring, BCC, M&E, and in-country capacity building. For certain intervention activities, such as procurement of commodities, training, and BCC, PMI focuses its efforts on 14 prefectures and the 5 communes of Conakry at the request of the NMCP, while the remaining prefectures are covered by Global Fund. A guiding principle of PMI's strategy is to support the population of Guinea through the most efficient and effective use of its resources, and PMI is considered a principal and credited partner by the NMCP. In order to achieve results, PMI support will utilize a variety of partners, but will focus efforts on one large, bilateral program that will be charged with building capacity in many of these areas. PMI will also provide technical assistance through the presence of two Resident Advisors who will work closely on a day-to-day basis with the NMCP to help build their capacity and improve national program performance. Headquarters staff will provide additional assistance in specific technical areas such as M&E, entomology, and diagnostics.

PMI support includes:

- Procurement and delivery of LLINs to the district level (mass distribution and routine distribution);
- BCC activities to increase knowledge and use of malaria commodities among the general population;
- Support for training of health workers and CHWs on malaria in pregnancy (MIP) and case management;
- Improvement in integrated, clinical supervision at health centers, health posts, and community levels;
- Provision of key case management commodities including RDTs, ACTs, SP, and injectable artesunate;
- Capacity-building for lab staff to support and improve diagnostic capacity;
- Provision of microscopes for hospitals and quality control for microscopy;
- Continued support for the pharmaceutical system to strengthen the logistics and information management system, pharmaceutical system reform, and improvement of drug regulation capacity;
- Entomological support for monitoring and surveillance of vectors and capacity-building for entomologists; and
- Support for M&E at the district, regional, and national levels, including routine system strengthening, surveillance, data use for decision-making, and periodic household and health facility surveys.

PMI will continue to look for opportunities to support the national strategy, which may include better communication and coordination with private sector players, as they are the primary means by which Guineans obtain health services, as well as participating in a national-level coordination council to ensure transparency and synergy with key partners like the Global Fund.

OPERATIONAL PLAN

Prevention

Insecticide-Treated Nets

NMCP/PMI objectives

The 2013-2017 National Malaria Control Strategy currently calls for two universal coverage campaigns, one in 2013 and another in 2016 with a definition of universal coverage as one ITN per two persons. Starting in 2014, the strategy targets pregnant women and children less than one year old for routine distribution through ANC and the Expanded Program for Immunization (EPI). Currently, however, the NMCP has no plan for routine distribution through EPI. Until such a plan has been elaborated, PMI will target routine distribution to pregnant women through ANC. The strategy has not been finalized and PMI will work with the NMCP to ensure it is consistent with global targets and guidelines.

Progress during the last 12 months

The 2013 universal coverage campaign is taking place in two phases. Phase one took place during May in the Global Fund-targeted prefectures. The second phase will occur in the PMI targeted zones (14 prefectures and five communes of Conakry) but has been put off until October 2013 due to contracting and commodity procurement issues. During the May campaign, the GOG and partners distributed over 3.2 million LLINs in 19 prefectures with over 98% of campaign coupons recovered. A post campaign coverage survey will be conducted later this year. With FY 2011 and FY 2012 funds, PMI procured 1,590,000 LLINs for distribution in the 2013 campaign. Approximately 237,000 of the PMI-procured nets were used to cover the gap in nets needed during the first campaign phase, and the remainder will be distributed in October. Other partners (IDB, Japan and UNICEF) have provided nets to help cover the gap in the latter phase of the campaign. The magnitude of any remaining net gap in the second phase of the campaign will not be known until after the enumeration exercise is complete. The final distribution phase, where the net gap would become apparent, will take place in Conakry, which has the lowest prevalence throughout the country (3% based on preliminary 2012 DHS results). In addition, reprogrammed FY 2013 funds are being used to cover the cost of transporting these LLINs to distribution sites, planning, training, supervision, and social mobilization/communication for the campaign's second phase.

A coordination committee for the national campaign, established in February 2012, included personnel from the MOH, NMCP, and partner organizations including Catholic Relief Services, *Faisons Ensemble*, Maternal and Child Health Integrated Program, WHO, UNICEF, Country Coordinating Mechanism, Plan Guinea, Population Service International, Helen Keller International, *Medecins sans Frontières*, Child Fund, and PMI in-country staff. This committee was established to ensure adequate support for the planning, coordination, implementation, and evaluation of the 2013 national campaign.

Challenges, opportunities, and threats

Although the original intent was to have one massive campaign, the delay of the distribution in the PMI targeted zones allowed the NMCP and the implementing partners to learn lessons and gain insights from the strengths and weaknesses of the first phase. Some of the recommendations included reinforcing communication activities related to the distribution, especially for the actual method of distribution (coupons); increasing the number of days over which the distribution should occur; and decreasing the distance between beneficiaries and distribution points.

Commodity gap analysis

PMI will provide 180,000 LLINs for routine distribution, which will cover about 73% of the need for pregnant women in the PMI zones. The NMCP recently adopted provision of LLINs through EPI, but has no plan yet for distribution since the EPI program has not started in Guinea. The NMCP estimated that the 2015 routine net need for children under 5 attending EPI is approximately 2,054,545. Until the NMCP develops a distribution plan for EPI, all LLINs purchased for routine distribution will go to pregnant women during their first ANC visit. The PMI in-country team will continue to work with the NMCP to develop a routine distribution plan for EPI.

Routine LLIN Needs and Contributions	2013	2014	2015
Estimated population	11,414,149	11,767,987	12,132,795
Total number of potential pregnant women attending ANC	436,591	476,603	491,378
Total LLIN needs	0*	476,603	491,378
LLIN from Global Fund	0	Unknown	Unknown
LLIN from PMI	0	180,000	180,000
Gap in routine LLINs	0	296,603	311,378

*Due to 2013 Universal coverage campaign.

Assumptions: Population growth is estimated at 3.1% and based on 2009 population data. Approximately 4.5% of the population could become pregnant. Target for ANC attendance (i.e., IPTp 1) is 85% in 2013 and 90% in 2014 and 2015. Estimates are based on one LLIN for each potentially pregnant woman attending ANC. The need in 2013 is estimated to be zero given the universal coverage campaign. PMI proposes to contribute to covering the gap in PMI target zones only (estimated at 50% of the total population).

Plans and justifications

With FY 2014 funds, PMI proposes to provide funds to procure 180,000 LLINs to revive the system for routine distribution through ANC visits. Although the national strategy includes coverage with LLINs for routine services and health facilities have distributed ITNs during ANC visits in the past, very few ITNs have been available for such activities recently. PMI will work with the NMCP and partners to improve the routine system to ensure delivery of ITNs to facilities as they need them, as well as support training around a package of services provided during routine visits. PMI will work the NMCP and partners to improve the routine system and ensure delivery of nets to the facilities that need them.

Proposed activities with FY 2014 funding: ($790,000)

1. *Procurement and delivery of LLINs:* Procure and deliver 180,000 LLINs for ANC in the PMI target zones. This funding will include the cost of the nets and delivery to the district level in the PMI target areas (*$610,000*);

2. *Distribution of LLINs*: Distribute180,000 LLINs from district to community health facilities in PMI targeted prefectures *($180,000);* and

3. *BCC for LLIN use*: Continue to promote LLIN use as part of the integrated communication strategy following national guidelines and in collaboration with other partners (*costs covered in BCC section*).

Indoor Residual Spraying

NMCP/PMI objectives

The 2013-2017 National Malaria Control Strategy describes IRS as one of their vector control interventions. They plan to achieve 80% coverage in targeted districts, but the targeted zones were not named and no selection method has been described. IRS is not currently part of the PMI strategy in Guinea.

Progress during the last 12 months

Very limited IRS activities are carried out in the districts Boke, Lola, Boffa, and Siguiri (less than 2% coverage) – all areas with extensive mining. The mining companies, Rio Tinto and Vale have dedicated funds for malaria control interventions including IRS, but in most cases the IRS is limited to camps and/or the houses of their workers.

PMI funded a 10 day training course for 24 entomology personnel including entomologists from the MOH (4 at the NMCP, 1 at the National Public Health Laboratory, 1 at the National Directorate of Public Hygiene and 3 at the center for research in Maferinyah) and 2 entomological technicians from each of 7 prefectures. Mosquito surveys and limited insecticide susceptibility assays were carried out in September 2012 in Boffa. The principal vector collected was *An. gambiae s.l.*, and preliminary data suggest the presence of mosquitoes that are resistant to the following pyrethroids: deltamethrine, lambda-cyhalothrine and permethrine. No other insecticide classes were tested.

Challenges, opportunities, and threats

A lack of qualified personnel, infrastructure, and funds will hinder the development of an IRS program. In addition, insecticide resistance has been detected, including in the areas that have been sprayed by the mining companies.

At least seven entomologists are employed by the MOH with considerable experience in vector-borne disease monitoring. Nevertheless, entomological monitoring capacity is very limited due to a lack of resources (e.g., no vehicles, trapping equipment, or insectary). The PMI implementing partner will help facilitate capacity building of the NMCP entomological staff, which will include linking them with existing technical capacity in the region, namely the Entomological Research Center in Cotonou, led by Dr. Martin Akogbeto.

Plans and justifications

The NMCP has expressed a desire to begin IRS operations in the country, but given the critical needs for LLINs and ACTs, PMI does not plan to support IRS activities with FY 2014 funding. PMI will continue to support standard entomological assessments including species identification, density, behavior and biting rates, as well as insecticide resistance assays since insecticide-based control interventions (LLINs) are being implemented in the country. Currently the plans include monitoring entomological parameters in one sentinel site in each of the four ecological zones of Guinea and establishing a collaborative agreement with a local research laboratory or university for the analysis of mosquito samples including insecticide resistance mechanisms.

Proposed activities with FY 2014 funding: ($175,000)

1. *Entomologic monitoring and capacity building:* Continued support for surveillance of vectors and insecticide resistance in each of the four ecological zones, capacity building for entomologists, and planning for the establishment of a permanent insectary. *($150,000);* and

2. *Technical assistance for entomological capacity building:* Support for two technical assistance visits from Centers for Disease Control and Prevention (CDC) to continue assistance to develop entomologic capacity *($25,000)*.

Malaria in Pregnancy

NMCP/PMI objectives

The NMCP adopted IPTp as a national policy in 2005. In 2013, the NMCP will finalize revisions of its national strategy and adopt current WHO recommendations for SP dosing and LLIN distribution, which are IPTp at each ANC visit and an LLIN given at the first ANC visit. Once the strategy is adopted, they will update national policy documents to reflect the changes. This change in policy will meet the needs of both non-HIV positive and HIV positive pregnant women. According to the national strategy, women of reproductive age represent 4.5% of the population, which is the percentage that the NMCP uses to quantify needs for SP and routine LLIN distribution through ANC. PMI will work with the NMCP to correct this so that the base statistic used to calculate needs is more reflective of the actual number of pregnancies that occur in one year.

According to national policy, the first SP treatment is delivered beginning at the 16th week of pregnancy. All IPTp are directly observed by the health worker. The NMCP target is that by 2014, 90% of pregnant women will have received at least 1 SP treatment, and 80% will have received 2 treatments. By 2015, this indicator will be 90% and 85%, respectively, for IPTp1 and IPTp2. The draft national strategy does not define any indicators to measure the proportion of pregnant women who sleep under an LLIN. The only LLIN target for pregnant women is that by 2014, 60% receive an LLIN during an ANC visit, which increases to 70% in 2015. PMI will work with the NMCP to revise the draft strategy to ensure that it is in line with WHO recommendations including relevant indicators, before it is validated. The revisions should include an indicator and target for IPTp3 since quantifications for SP needs are based on three treatments.

Progress during last 12 months

The preliminary data from the 2012 DHS showed that while 85% of women make at least one ANC visit, only 18% receive 2 or more doses IPTp (up from 3% in the 2005 DHS). Implementation of IPTp has been hampered by stockouts of SP over the past 2 years, which may explain the slow progress in reaching targets, as the 2013 target of 80% of pregnant women receiving IPTp1 will likely be missed. On a positive note, the most recent end-use verification survey (EUV) showed only 3 of 18 facilities with SP stockouts on the day of the visit (April 2013), which may indicate that the situation is improving. Preliminary DHS data showed that 28% of pregnant women slept under an LLIN the previous night, up from 1.4% in the 2005 DHS. It should be noted that no LLINs have been available for routine distribution for several years, so this number may be a reflection of the LLINs that were distributed nationwide for vulnerable groups, in 2009, including women of reproductive age and children under five.

As part of ongoing support to the national strategy, PMI procured 375,000 SP treatments for distribution. This consignment was distributed nationwide rather than in PMI zones alone due to the delay in disbursing Global Fund resources during the consolidation and revising of the 2006 and 2010 grants, which had planned to purchase and distribute SP in their zones. The plan moving forward will be to have PMI procure and distribute SP for the entire country. This gap in previously planned support most likely contributed to stockouts of SP that were recorded in the last year, which may be one of the factors contributing to the low IPTp coverage seen in the preliminary DHS data.

PMI provided support for training and supervision of health facility workers in IPTp and communication messages for increasing knowledge and promoting prevention of MIP at the community level. Across the PMI target zones, 419 health facility workers and 206 CHWs were trained on malaria case management, including MIP. Also, 58 supervisors from the central, regional, and prefectural levels were trained in supervision, although what portion of these supervisors carried out supervisory visits post-training remains unclear. Finally, there were over 169,000 people reached via home visits and community-level activities such as group discussions. Although all PMI zones received training, not all health facility staff were trained, nor were all potential beneficiaries reached with messages. These activities were stopped in December 2012 in anticipation of the start of a new bilateral program; however a delay in the award left a six-month gap, and only since June 2013 have training, supervision, and communication activities restarted.

Challenges, opportunities, and threats

The stockouts of SP over the past few years have hampered the implementation of IPTp as indicated by the low uptake (18%) of at least 2 doses of SP reported in the preliminary 2012 DHS results; although things may be improving as witnessed by recent EUV survey data. Also, limited involvement of private facilities in following the national strategy negatively impacts maximum IPTp coverage, since more than half of the population uses the private sector for health services.

The current national IPTp policy is not in line with the WHO guidelines for a less narrowly-defined dosing schedule for SP. The dosing guidelines based on gestational weeks may be confusing to health workers and contributing to low IPTp uptake. The new, national strategy for 2013-2017 is being developed in order to bring it in line with WHO recommendations. PMI will work with the NMCP to ensure that these revisions are made before the new strategy is adopted and that the MOH policy documents are also revised.

The absence of consumption data and a strong pharmaceutical and supply chain management system hinders the ability of the NMCP to accurately forecast needs and manage supplies, even when drugs become available. With continuing PMI support for integrated case management training and supply of essential diagnostic and drug commodities, the human and logistical resource capacity for IPTp should improve. Increased advocacy for an MIP policy revision that is more in line with WHO guidelines, awareness-raising, referral, and utilization of IPTp by health facility and community workers as well as community members should help improve key MIP indicators.

Commodity gap analysis

With an estimated national population of over 12 million and the proportion of women of reproductive age being 4.5%, it is estimated that 545,976 pregnancies could occur in 2015. PMI will procure approximately 1,437,500 treatments of SP to meet approximately 98% of the nationwide need.

SP Needs and Contributions	2013	2014	2015
Estimated population	11,414,149	11,767,987	12,132,795
Total number of potential pregnant women attending ANC	436,591	476,603	491,378
Total SP needs	1,309,773	1,429,810	1,474,135
SP from PMI	375,000	375,000	1,437,500
SP from Global Fund	0	0	0
SP from IDB	50,000	0	0
Gap in SP	884,773	1,054,810	36,635

Assumptions: Population growth is estimated at 3.1% and based on 2009 population data. Approximately 4.5% of the population could become pregnant. Target for ANC attendance (i.e., IPTp 1) is 85% in 2013 and 90% in 2014 and 2015. The NMCP bases SP needs on 3 doses for each pregnant woman attending ANC. Due to relatively low cost of SP and no provision of SP by the Global Fund, PMI proposes to cover the nationwide needs for SP.

Plans and justifications

PMI will continue to support activities aimed at enhancing the provision of effective MIP services in public and private health facilities in Guinea. To that end, PMI will procure enough SP treatments to cover most of the estimated needs nationwide, as well as a portion of the LLIN need for routine distribution during ANC visits (see ITN section). Additionally, PMI will continue to support BCC training and messaging to improve the demand for ANC services and understanding of the benefits of IPTp among community members and health workers. PMI will support laboratory diagnosis and appropriate treatment of MIP to reinforce the implementation of MIP services, including training and supervision of IPTp service delivery along with other aspects of effective case management, and promotion of LLIN use. PMI will work with the MOH and NMCP who are prepared to update their strategy and policy documents with regard to MIP based upon WHO recommendations. The total FY 2014 funding that can be attributed to MIP is greater than the $62,500 listed in this section based on the activities listed above, the costs for which appear in those sections including ITNs for routine distribution, diagnostics, case management and BCC.

Proposed activities with FY 2014 funding: ($62,500)

1. *Procure treatments of SP:* Procure approximately 1,437,500 treatments of SP to cover all of the needs in Guinea for 2015 *($57,500)*;

2. *Procure supplies to ensure consumption of SP at ANC:* Procure supplies such as cups and water to ensure that SP is taken at the time of ANC visit *($5,000)*;

3. *Promote BCC for IPTp*: Promote ANC clinic attendance and educate pregnant women and communities on the benefits of IPTp. This activity will include support for community-level approaches, such as training of community-based workers, as well as mass media (including local radio stations). Immunization outreach sessions will be used as opportunities for educating women. This will be part of a larger integrated BCC activity to satisfy needs for case management, LLINs, and IPTp *(Costs covered in BCC section)*;

4. *Provide training/refresher training for MIP*: Provide training and refresher training for public and private health facility midwives and nurses to correctly deliver SP in the context of the focused ANC approach. Training will include benchmark assessments, on-the-job training of the new treatment algorithm, and coaching. Training will be part of an integrated training package *(Costs covered in Case Management/Diagnosis section)*; and

5. *Supervise health workers in IPTp to improve quality of service:* Provide on-site supervision for public health facility midwives and nurses to correctly deliver SP in the context of the focused ANC approach. Supervision will continue to be part of an integrated approach for supervision at health facilities *(Costs covered in Case Management/Diagnosis section)*.

Case Management

Diagnosis

<u>NMCP/PMI objectives</u>

The NMCP strategy and national policy recommends diagnostic confirmation of all suspected malaria cases among all patients aged five years and older, with either microscopy (only in hospitals) or an RDT before they are treated. However, the NMCP endorses the WHO recommendation of diagnostic confirmation for suspect malaria cases among patients of *all ages*, which will be included in the revised strategy and policy documents before the end of this year. According to the policy RDTs are provided free of charge and will be widely used at public health facilities and by CHWs, while microscopy services incur a fee.

According to Guinea's health services package, all hospitals and health centers should provide microscopy services; however, a Global Fund-financed health facility survey of hospitals and health centers in 2010 showed that fewer than half the facilities in Guinea had a microscope (approximately 100% of hospitals but only 40% of health centers).[11] Microscopes often are not functional and health facilities may lack reagents and consumables. Data from the health facility survey indicated that only 43% of hospitals and health centers had slides, and 19% had Giemsa stain. Staff from the NMCP and the National Laboratory, which is part of the National Institute of Public Health, are responsible for supervision of microscopy, although no comprehensive quality assurance/quality control program has been developed for malaria.

The NMCP also supports the use of RDTs for malaria diagnosis at all levels of the health care system. According to the Global Fund health facility survey, 34% of health facilities had RDTs in 2010. In addition to rolling out RDTs in health facilities, the NMCP would like to roll out RDTs at the community level through CHWs. Capacity building through training on the use of RDTs, ACTs, IPTp, and BCC for health workers and CHWs is a key part of this intervention.

Progress during the last 12 months

During the last 12 months, PMI supported the development of the updated national strategy and policy which includes important revisions on the use of diagnostics to confirm suspect malaria cases before treatment. In support of the new policy, PMI procured 1.1 million RDTs for the PMI target zones. Of these, 100,000 were used to cover training needs for health workers and CHWs and by trained CHWs for malaria diagnosis at the community level. The remaining 1 million RDTs were distributed by PMI to facilities. PMI is also in the process of procuring microscopes and consumables for select health facilities.

PMI supported a rapid laboratory assessment in March 2012 and found that most facilities do not have a functional microscope; only thick smears tend to be performed; and only 30% of facilities perform RDTs. In those facilities with RDTs, different brands are in use, and the assessment found no evidence of guidance, protocols, or job aids. The partner used the assessment findings to inform activities including a nationwide training of 62 laboratory technicians in malaria

---

[11] This was a nationally-representative survey with a sample of 129 health facilities.

diagnosis, including microscopy maintenance, supply management, and RDT use. Using the trained laboratory technicians, PMI supported additional training of 771 health facility clinicians and CHWs in RDT use at the facility and community levels. PMI also provided technical support to the NMCP to develop materials for organizing and conducting refresher training courses in diagnostics.

PMI has supported supervision of health workers – including diagnostics for case management – at the hospital, health center, and health post levels, as well as of CHWs at the community level. PMI also supported the revision and validation of a guide for community case management of malaria, as well as a training manual for activity organizers on malaria prevention and treatment.

Challenges, opportunities, and threats

The delay in the validation of the NMCP's new national strategy poses a challenge for formalizing the new diagnostics policies, as training and commodities for diagnostic confirmation are rolled out throughout the country. A lack of RDTs in many health facilities also makes it difficult for health workers to fulfill the new national policy. The lack of strong pharmaceutical and commodities supply chain management and logistical management information system makes it difficult for the NMCP to generate reliable data on consumption, supply, needs, and distribution of commodities. In addition, the low capacity and motivation of some CHWs and Health and Hygiene Committee members, along with high turnover among health facility workers threatens the country's ability to grow a cadre of experienced and trained health care providers.

As RDTs and training continue to be rolled out to multiple levels in the health system, the problems described above are improving. In the future, with additional training and supervision, health facilities will hopefully increase their ability to collect consumption data and use those data to mitigate the risk of stockouts and expiration of commodities procured by donors.

Commodity gap analysis

The table below presents RDTs needs for 2013, 2014 and 2015, as specified by the gap analysis conducted by the NMCP. PMI plans to procure enough RDTs to cover approximately 76% of the total need in the PMI target zones. The country is trying to find other donors to fill the gaps. In the past they have received support from the IDB and the Japanese government. Currently, UNICEF is planning to procure RDTs as well.

RDT Needs and Contributions	2013	2014	2015
Estimated population	11,414,149	11,767,987	12,132,795
Total RDT needs	11,176,734	11,523,214	11,880,432
Total RDT needs in PMI target zone	5,588,367	5,761,607	5,940,216
RDTs from PMI	4,000,000	5,000,000	4,515,000
RDTs from Global Fund	1,111,803	4,436,615	Unknown
RDTs from IDB	335,000	Unknown	Unknown
RDTs gap	5,729,931	2,086,599	7,365,432

Assumptions: Population growth is estimated at 3.1% and based on 2009 population data. The number of fevers per person per year is estimated to be 1.6 based on a 2009 survey conducted in preparation for Global Fund Round10. The percent of the population seeking any health care for fever is estimated at 90%; 60% of these go to a public health facility and 8% seek care at the community level. PMI proposes to contribute to covering the gap in PMI target zones only (approximately 50% of the total population).

Plans and justification

PMI will continue to support the NMCP's national policy of malaria case management based on diagnostic confirmation by supporting scale up of RDT use and strengthen microscopy through provision of commodities, as well as training and supervision at the health facility and community levels. Commodity procurement and training will be focused in the PMI target zones. Training and supervision will continue to provide long-term, ongoing support to strengthen diagnostic services at all levels of the health care system by identifying areas that require improvement and providing on-site feedback and technical advice and support to the front-line clinicians and laboratory staff in peripheral health facilities. Training and supervision for diagnostics will be integrated with community case management as well as other malaria prevention and care activities. PMI will not plan to use microscopy to assess the quality of RDTs, rather PMI plans to work to ensure that tests are performed correctly to improve quality of testing through training, supervision, and job aids. One specific component of diagnostic strengthening will be investment in development of a comprehensive quality assurance and quality control system for microscopy and RDTs. This will ensure sustainable gains and country capacity building in diagnostic practices.

Proposed activities with FY 2014 funding: ($4,010,000)

1. *Procure rapid diagnostics tests (RDTs):* Procure approximately 4,515,000 RDTs to continue scaling up RDT use in health facilities and in communities via CHWs *($2,800,000);*

2. *Procure microscopes and consumables:* Procure 15 microscopes, reagents, slides, and repair materials for hospitals as well as reagents, slides, and repair materials for previously purchased microscopes *($50,000);*

3. *Improved malaria diagnostics:* Work with the NMCP and National Laboratory to develop and support a comprehensive quality assurance and quality control plan for malaria diagnostics at all levels of the health system. This will include refresher training

for lab technicians (and training on malaria microscopy for new laboratory technicians) and regular supervision of microscopy and RDT performance, including systematic review of a predetermined number of positive and negative blood smears and simultaneous use of both tests to assess the quality of RDTs in diagnosing malaria *($200,000);*

4. *Provide training/refresher training in RDT use:* Provide refresher training on malaria diagnostics, including correct RDT use at all levels of the health care system. The new national policy concerning use of diagnosis has been revised and that's why it is necessary to carry out refresher training for those who have already been trained and continue to train new health workers. The revision of the new policy takes into account community aspects, which will emphasize the supervisory activities of health workers for policy compliance and behavior change. The new direction in the policy takes into account all aspects of community and therefore more CHWs to be trained. Community case management is a new activity in Guinea, we believe that a cautious approach at the beginning, is more appropriate, thus a smaller budget to start scale up, and a larger project to train personnel. New health care workers and CHWs will be trained with FY 2013 funding. This will be an integrated RDT/case management training *($600,000);* and

5. *Supervise health workers and CHWs in RDT use*: Provide integrated, regular supervision of health workers and CHWs focusing on microscopy and RDT performance. (This will be integrated RDT/case management supervision) *($360,000).*

Treatment

NMCP/PMI objectives

As described in the *Diagnostics* section, in accordance with WHO guidelines, the MOH requires mandatory confirmation of suspect malaria cases before treatment administration. This requirement applies to both forms of malaria (uncomplicated and severe) and at all levels of the health system including the community level.

In Guinea, the first-line ACT for uncomplicated malaria is artesunate-amodiaquine (AS-AQ) with artemether-lumefantrine as the second line treatment, prescribed in cases of treatment failure, side effects, or intolerance to AS-AQ. These recommendations apply to health facilities in all sectors and at all levels of the health system. At the community level, only the first-line treatment (AS-AQ) is used. In cases of AS-AQ intolerance, side effects, or treatment failure, the patient should be referred to the nearest health facility. Per national policy, pregnant women in their first trimester with uncomplicated malaria are to be treated with oral quinine; in the second and third trimesters, they are to be treated with AS-AQ. Both the first- and second-line ACTs are free for adults and children (as are RDTs), but patients have to pay for other malaria drugs received, as well as for microscopy tests.

As stated in the revised draft strategy, the first choice for treatment of severe malaria is intravenous or intramuscular artesunate. Other acceptable treatments include injectable artemether or quinine.

28

Progress during the last 12 months

In 2012 in response to widespread stockouts of ACTs at many health facilities, the NMCP requested support from PMI in procuring ACTs to be used in health facilities and at the community level. PMI, through its implementing partners, ensured a nationwide distribution of ACTs in November 2012. Over 400 health centers, hospitals and some military clinics benefitted directly from the distribution of ACTs, a portion of which were also distributed to CHWs. In an effort to avoid future stockouts and the need for further emergency ACT procurements, PMI has supported implementation of new strategies to estimate treatment needs. PMI and partners, including the NMCP, have since introduced monthly reporting forms and tools to ensure a more consistent flow of information from the health facility to the district level, and up to the central level. Moving forward, health facilities will be re-supplied with malaria products after sending monthly reports detailing the number of medicines given to patients. The data will allow NMCP and the MOH to plan the distribution of the proper quantity of products to the local level and how much to acquire for the country as a whole better, reducing the risk of shortages.

PMI also procured 50,000 ampoules of injectable quinine for treating severe malaria cases and supported the revision of the national guidelines which included the adoption of the WHO recommendation for the use of injectable artesunate for severe malaria cases.

Challenges, opportunities, and threats

Although some remarkable improvements were observed this year, shortages of ACTs continue to be a problem, as evidenced by the most recent EUV survey (April 2013) where 4 out of 20 facilities experienced stockouts on the day the survey was conducted. One of the most important challenges is the lack of an efficient pharmaceutical supply chain system resulting in many commodities being bottlenecked at the central level and an inability to accurately forecast needs and track supply. Donors, especially the European Union (EU), are working to coordinate efforts and influence the management of the pharmaceutical system to improve transparency and accountability. The EU carried out an audit for the Central Pharmacy of Guinea (PCG) and the resulting recommendations will soon be made available. Donors, including PMI, will be closely monitoring the country's adoption and implementation of the recommendations as an indicator that the PCG is taking a more proactive approach to strengthening the pharmaceutical system.

An additional challenge is the quality of malaria treatments available in the private (unregulated) sector. The source, effectiveness, and storage conditions of these medications are unknown, and the GOG has no control over this parallel market. This issue poses a threat not only to the health of Guineans who may be receiving sub-optimal treatment for malaria, but to the effectiveness of viable antimalarials in the face of potential resistance. PMI will work with the NMCP and MOH as well as other key partners to develop a strategy on how to gather information on the private sector.

The Maferinyah Training and Research Center is currently conducting therapeutic efficacy studies for AS-AQ and testing efficacy of alternative ACTs in clinical trials. Not only are these incredibly useful data for ensuring effective treatment of malaria cases, but it is important that this research capacity exists in country to conduct future research on treatment effectiveness. PMI will consider funding therapeutic efficacy studies if needed in the future depending on the outcome of current studies being conducted by Maferinyah. PMI will continue to communicate with the Maferinyah researchers and the NMCP to ensure therapeutic efficacy study work continues on a timeline that is consistent with PMI guidance.

There is lack of skilled human resources in the case management unit at the NMCP, as well as in some peripheral health facilities and at the community level. But as the NMCP continues to develop its capacity, particularly under the leadership of the Coordinator and Deputy Coordinator, and financial and technical partners continue to strengthen the control program in Guinea, human resource capacity at all levels of the health system will continue to improve.

Commodity gap analysis

The table below presents ACT needs for 2013, 2014, and 2015, as specified by the gap analysis conducted by the NMCP. PMI plans to procure enough ACTs to cover approximately 77% of the total need in the PMI target zones.

ACTs Needs and Contributions	2013	2014	2015
Estimated population	11,414,149	11,767,987	12,132,795
Total ACT needs	4,470,694	4,609,285	4,752,173
Total ACT needs in PMI target zone	2,235,347	2,304,643	2,376,087
ACTs from PMI	1,440,000	2,000,000	1,833,000
ACTs from Global Fund	1,001,742	2,043,171	1,146,695
Gap in ACTs	2,028,952	566,114	1,772,478

Assumptions: Population growth is estimated at 3.1% and based on 2009 population data. ACT needs are based on a 40% RDT positivity rate. See RDT gap analysis table for assumptions about quantifying RDT needs. PMI proposes to contribute to covering the gap in PMI target zones only (estimated at 50% of the total population).

The table below presents injectable artesunate needs for 2013, 2014, and 2015, as specified by the gap analysis conducted by the NMCP. PMI plans to procure enough injectable artesunate to cover approximately 100% of the need in the PMI target zones.

Injectable Artesunate Needs and Contributions	2013	2014	2015
Estimated population	11,414,149	11,767,987	12,132,795
Total injectable artesunate needs	134,121	138,279	142,565
Total injectable artesunate needs in PMI target zones	67,061	69,139	71,283
Injectable artesunate from PMI	130,000	69,000	71,000
Injectable artesunate from Global Fund	0	0	0
Gap in injectable artesunate	4,121	69,279	71,565

Assumptions: Population growth is estimated at 3.1% and based on 2009 population data. Injectable artesunate needs are based on the assumption that 3% of the 40% of tested cases confirmed positive are cases of severe malaria. PMI proposes to contribute to covering the gap in PMI target zones only (estimated at 50% of the total population).

Plans and justification

As it is stated in the new strategy, PMI will continue to procure ACTs for all age groups in the PMI target zones to support appropriate treatment based on laboratory diagnosis. To facilitate the distribution of ACTs, PMI will procure and deliver them down to lowest level necessary to ensure that they reach beneficiaries. Additionally, PMI will procure the injectable artesunate to cover needs in the PMI target zones for severe malaria cases.

PMI plans to support integrated BCC activities to promote appropriate treatment-seeking behavior among community members. Human capacity building will continue to be a part of this intervention through clinical and refresher training in malaria case management for all age groups and vulnerable populations, and supervision of health workers and CHWs. PMI is planning to train 655 health workers and CHWs, identified in PMI target zones. Previously, 419 health workers and 206 CHWs were trained in case management. Rough estimates indicate that we will be reaching about 75% of health workers within the PMI zones. Ultimately, the plan is to train every health worker and CHW in our target zones, but work needs to be done to support the MOH to get a better handle on the total work force throughout the country so that we can determine how close we are to full coverage. The Global Fund will be doing similar training in their target zones.

Scale-up of community case management will also include management, logistic, and data management support. As the move to SMS picks up, PMI will work with partners to ensure that data being gathered is analyzed and used to inform decisions and better assess needs for supplies, case detection, and treatment at the community level.

Proposed activities with FY 2014 funding: $1,300,000

1. *Procure and distribute ACTs:* Procure and distribute approximately 1,833,000 ACTs *($990,000)*;

2. *Procurement of injectable artesunate*: Fund procurement of 71,300 treatments of injectable artesunate for severe malaria *($180,000)*;

3. *BC) for case management*: Fund integrated BCC and education activities for communities to improve behaviors related to malaria prevention and treatment. The BCC supported in 2014 will target prevention activities, including use of LLINs and IPTp. BCC activities will also support appropriate care seeking behaviors, with particular emphasis placed on prompt care-seeking for fever and other symptoms of malaria *(cost covered under BCC section)*;

31

4. *Clinical training/refresher training in malaria case management:* Integrated refresher training in RDT use, malaria case management, and MIP for health workers at hospitals, health centers, and health posts trained using previous years' funds. Training of CHWs not yet trained in RDT use, treatment of uncomplicated malaria, referral for patients with severe malaria, and referral of pregnant women to ANCs. Continue implementation of a comprehensive refresher training schedule for health workers and CHWs who have already received initial training *(Cost covered under Case Management/Diagnosis section)*;

5. *Supervision of health workers and CHWs*: Enhance clinical supervision at all levels of the health care system, including hospitals, health centers, health posts, and CHWs. District Health Team staff (*Direction Préfectorale de Santé*) and regional health team staff (*Direction Régionale de Santé*) will be actively involved in supervision activities, along with health center staff for supervision of CHWs. At the regional and prefecture levels, there will be one supervision visit per trimester. This level includes 8 regional and municipal hospitals, about 688 health posts and health centers, and 16 district hospitals. This represents about half of the nationwide total, since PMI supports approximately half of the country, with Global Fund supporting the other half. At the national level there will be two supervision visits per semester, covering two university hospitals. The plan is to support visits to all public facilities within the PMI target zones. Supervision visits will include observation of patient consultations and feedback to providers *(Cost covered under Case Management/Diagnosis section)*; and

6. *Community case management:* Support the scale-up of community case management in PMI target areas, including management and logistic costs, support for data management, and training of 650 CHWs *($130,000)*.

Pharmaceutical Management

NMCP/PMI objectives

The specific objective set forth in the new malaria national strategic plan is for the pharmaceutical system to provide treatment to 100% of patients. This overall objective implies supplying drugs to the health facilities on a national level in sufficient quantities and on a permanent basis.

Situation analysis:
The key player of the pharmaceutical system in Guinea is PCG. Created in 1992 by the GOG to supply the health facilities nationwide with quality drugs in appropriate quantities and in a timely manner, PCG operates under the administrative oversight of the National Directorate of Pharmacies and Laboratory (DNPL). PCG has established pharmaceutical depots in five of the eight regions in Guinea. This institution has also played a role as sub-recipient of Global Fund grants to procure drugs for the three priority diseases (HIV, Tuberculosis, and malaria). Despite its storage capacity of 4,455 square meters across the country, 3,815 of which are available in Conakry, PCG continues to struggle to fulfill its responsibilities.

Since its creation in 1992, PCG has engaged in a decentralization policy to ensure that health commodities are distributed to health facilities in the most effective manner, but its performance during the last five years has been problematic. As a result, to date, only five regional depots (Conakry, Labe, Faranah, Kankan, and N'Zerekore) have been created, making the remaining three regions (Kindia, Boke, and Mamou) dependent on the Central Warehouse in Conakry or on a neighboring depot. A sixth depot has recently been created in Boke, but has yet to be equipped. Various assessments have been conducted by donors including United States Agency for International Development (USAID) and PMI over the past five years to identify bottlenecks in PCG development and assist with addressing them in order to improve the performance of the supply chain and the pharmaceutical system. More recently, the EU has sponsored an audit of PCG and the pharmaceutical system. The report of the audit has not yet been made public.

Guinea has 387 private pharmacies nationwide of which about 70% are located in Conakry. A multitude of non-registered businesses also sell pharmaceutical products, with many of them serving as the only commercial outlet in a particular rural area. Those pharmacies sell a wide range of antimalarial drugs, including both branded and generic drugs. The price range of these drugs in the private pharmacies is between $0.53 per treatment for generic drugs to $14 per treatment for branded drugs. To supply the private pharmacies, at least 35 wholesale distributors operate in the country, all of which are based in Conakry.

According to the national pharmaceutical policy, the national essential drugs list should be revised every two years, but that is not being done on a regular basis. PMI's partner is supporting the DNPL to streamline the process of revising the list on a regular basis.

Progress during the last 12 months

Since its launch in FY 2011, PMI has clearly identified the PCG as the main institution to strengthen in order to ensure a smooth distribution of drugs to end users. In the absence of a convention between the NMCP and PCG, PMI's partner worked on a temporary solution to distribute a new tranche of products for approximately four months to the districts. Antimalarial drugs were directly delivered to health officials during a meeting held in Conakry. Distribution of ACTs was done based on monthly consumption reports since November 2012, while the other products were allocated in equal quantities to the health facilities because of long stockout periods leading to the impossibility of calculating the average monthly consumption. The quantification and distribution process was closely coordinated with the NMCP and PCG.

One of the main targets of the past 12 months was to guide the NMCP and PCG in establishing and agreeing on how the routine distribution of PMI products to the regions can continue. The importance of such an agreement is reflected by the need to avoid emergency distributions caused by frequent stockouts throughout the country and to encourage the smooth functioning of the supply side, in addition to the demand side (as represented by good reporting and product orders from facilities). In June 2013 the NMCP and PCG signed a memorandum of understanding to guide the storage, management, and distribution of PMI products to the regions. A similar memorandum of understanding exists for Global Fund products; however, the Global Fund is just starting to deliver products in Guinea again after a long break, and the products, with the exception of ACTs, will be distributed in non-PMI zones. By supporting such a memorandum of understanding, PMI wanted to ensure an efficient supply chain management system in Guinea and ultimately the success of the PMI program.

PMI currently supports the DNPL in the development of an implementation plan for Guinea's National Pharmaceutical Policy. This work has been initiated and will continue this year through a series of development and validation meetings. Also, the essential drugs list has been updated with PMI support and will be closely monitored by the DNPL.

During the past 12 months, 2 EUV surveys were conducted; the results of the first were disseminated to major stakeholders, while those of the second are currently being finalized.

Challenges, opportunities, and threats

The PCG is not currently capable of ensuring that drugs imported by PMI or other donors supporting malaria are appropriately distributed and made available for use in the health system in a timely manner. A technical assistance package being provided by PMI to strengthen the supply chain and the pharmaceutical system management is yet to be understood and used by the PCG authorities to achieve the desired results, as strong resistance remains to activities geared towards improving governance of PCG.

The GOG is struggling to eradicate an illicit network for essential drugs in Guinea. Drugs purchased in the market are less expensive, and patients buy these drugs regardless of the quality and effectiveness of the medication. As much as 40% of the drugs available in the health facilities originate in the market and are sold to patients by nurses and midwives acting as middlemen.

The legal and regulatory environment of the pharmaceutical system also needs improvement, as revealed by many assessments. From the last MOP visit conducted in Guinea, it became apparent during the PMI team's discussion with PCG's officials that they are resistant to reforms that will lead to improving the legal status of the PCG and create conditions for a strong and well-performing supply chain. The current practice that appeals to the Guinean authorities is to sign a memorandum of understanding with each donor that imports drugs into the country with such donor providing to PCG a percentage (3%-10%) of the value of imported drugs. There seems to be no interest in a comprehensive package of reforms that will contribute to improving the regulatory environment of PCG, and thus strengthen the supply chain with transparent procedures, although many donors including PMI and EU are willing to support such an undertaking.

Lack of transparency in the management of the PCG has prompted the EU to carry out an assessment and pledge to provide substantial support once recommendations are implemented. PMI and other partners fully support the EU in this initiative and have also pledged to support the PCG's operations once transparency standards are in place. Although recommendations have not yet been made public, the EU mentioned that most of them are related to governance issues (e.g., transparency in procurement operations, line of authorities, governing board, and representativeness of private sector and civil society). The EU would like to make the application of recommendations a condition for a $42 million project to strengthen the health system that will roll out in 2014.

The involvement of community groups in the health sector provides a firm foundation for increased community participation in the pharmaceutical system management. At the commune level, the Health and Hygiene committees are composed of citizens coming from surrounding villages, including women and men, who discuss health issues and participate in decision-making. This offers a potential opportunity for strengthening civil society's participation in improving the pharmaceutical system, by advocating for reducing stockouts and increasing transparency.

The March 2012 PMI-supported Round Table is still referred to by Guinean authorities as an opportunity as it has created a consensual platform that may help generate more commitment from the GOG in favor of the pharmaceutical system. Guinea has established a pharmaco-vigilance system, but it is not currently functional. The lack of a tracer mechanism for drugs at PCG, as well as in private wholesalers, represents a real threat to public health. Quality control of reagents and tests results is limited.

Plans and justification

The Guinea pharmaceutical system needs a great deal of attention and support from all stakeholders to address the multiple governance issues hindering its performance. Since 2011, PMI has been playing a leading role in supporting the pharmaceutical system. In collaboration with the implementing partners and other donors, PMI will closely monitor the implementation of activities planned in FY 2012 and FY 2013 MOPs to strengthen the pharmaceutical system. PMI will support establishment of a functional drugs quantification committee that will better identify commodity needs and guide procurement decisions nationwide.

PMI will maintain working relations with PCG and will abide by the EU audit recommendations to contribute to improving the governance of PCG and create conditions for supplying drugs to service delivery points nationwide. Meanwhile, PMI plans, in consultation with the Global Fund and other interested partners, to conduct an assessment of the commodities distribution circuit and use a temporary mechanism to supply drugs and other malaria commodities directly to districts and down to health facilities. This is not a parallel drugs supply system, but rather, interim measures to transfer drugs to service delivery points, while maintaining dialogue with the PCG.

Proposed activities with FY 2014 funding: ($1,250,000)

1. *Support for improving logistic management information systems*: Continue support to strengthen the logistic management information systems to enable the pharmaceutical system to collect, compile, and process consumption data throughout the health system in order to improve the forecasting, the procurement, and the distribution of commodities. This activity includes procurement of computers, support for internet connectivity, and capacity building for quantification at the central level (PCG, DNPL), as well as at the regional, prefecture, and district levels *($100,000)*;

2. *Support pharmaceutical systems reform*: Continue to support the reform of regulations governing the supply chain management and the pharmaceutical system, including the

implementation of the recommendations of the audit performed by the EU. Reforms are required not only at the central level but also to the periphery in how stocks are managed. PMI's support of the EU audit findings and recommendations will be linked to this activity *($250,000);* and

3. *Support to improve drug regulatory capacity*: Continue to support improvement of the regulatory and oversight capacities of the DNPL, revision of national list of essential drugs, and enhanced control of compliance to the pharmaceutical policy and regulations by PCG and the private pharmacies network. Capacity building of the pharmaceutical system will include improving capacity to combat counterfeit drugs and the illicit sale of drugs. Much of this work, too, will be informed by the EU audit findings and recommendations *($300,000)*.

4. *Support for management of pharmaceutical supplies*: Manage the distribution of PMI commodities down to the health facility level, including warehousing, transportation, storage and distribution *($600,000)*.

Monitoring & Evaluation and Operational Research

NMCP/PMI objectives

M&E is a key component of Guinea's malaria program, and the NMCP recognizes the importance of having a strong M&E strategy to inform programmatic interventions and measure outcomes and impact. In 2008, the NMCP developed a costed national M&E plan for the period of 2008-2012. It has worked to revise and update the plan for 2013-2017, but it has not yet been finalized. A priority activity for the new PMI bilateral project is to finalize the updated plan. The 2008-2012 plan identifies indicators, targets, and data sources and emphasizes data collection, data quality assurance, and dissemination and use of data. Specific M&E priorities that will be reflected in the updated plan include revising and maintaining the national malaria database, including the health management and information system (HMIS) and supervision data; creating and disseminating malaria bulletins; building M&E capacity at regional and district levels; and strengthening relationships with partners collecting malaria data, including HMIS and the Integrated Disease Surveillance and Response system.

Currently, the following data sources collect malaria data in Guinea:

Routine System
HMIS: The NMCP and HMIS seem to have a strong collaboration, as evidenced by recent changes to the routine HMIS reporting form to collect revised commodity and epidemiological data on the same form. Revised indicators include the number of suspect cases and confirmed cases. While the annual HMIS report is not currently perceived as a timely or valid data source on which to base programmatic decisions, gains have been made in revising routine reporting tools to collect needed malaria data.

Integrated Disease Surveillance and Response system: While potentially a timelier tool for routine malaria data (meant to report weekly the number of confirmed malaria cases), these data are typically inaccurate as diagnostic confirmation of cases is still relatively low due to incomplete roll out of RDTs on a national scale. It is not clear whether or not clinically diagnosed cases are included in Integrated Disease Surveillance and Response reporting.

Evaluation

Household surveys: Guinea has implemented a DHS in 2005, a MICS in 2007, and Global Fund-supported national coverage surveys conducted in 2009 and 2010 to measure population coverage with basic interventions (ITNs, IPTp, and ACTs), as well as a health facility component assessing commodity availability and case management practices.[12] Preliminary results from the 2012 DHS are currently available and should be finalized by August 2013; the 2012 DHS included the first national estimates of malaria parasitemia (as well as anemia). A Malaria Indicator Survey (MIS) is planned for 2014 and the next DHS will be implemented in 2017.

Health facility surveys: PMI has also proposed (and approved) a national health facility survey to be conducted in 2013. This survey will assess health facility readiness to provide effective malaria services, including diagnostic capacity and antimalarial drug stocks, as well as health worker case management practices. Because proper assessment of diagnostics and case management practices is dependent on availability of diagnostics commodities (i.e., RDTs), the survey will not be implemented until RDTs have been rolled out to all health facilities and health workers have been trained. It will be necessary for the NMCP and implementing partner to coordinate with the Global Fund principal recipient to ensure case management commodities and training are fully scaled up in the near future. The first EUV survey was implemented in late 2012 with the second one in April 2013.Timing of the health facility survey will be closely coordinated with future EUV surveys to avoid any duplication of data collection related to commodity stocks.

---

[12] The 2005 DHS data are available, but the 2007 MICS results are not maintained by UNICEF headquarters; they may be available in country. The reports from the 2009 and 2010 Global Fund surveys are available.

The table below summarizes malaria data sources in Guinea as well as anticipated data collection activities for the next five years.

Data Source	Year								
	2009	2010	2011	2012	2013	2014	2015	2016	2017
Household surveys	Nat'l coverage survey – Household module (Global Fund)*	Nat'l coverage survey – Household module (Global Fund)*		DHS (with parasitemia biomarkers)		MIS (proposed)			DHS
Other surveys	Nat'l coverage survey – Health Facility module (Global Fund)*	Nat'l coverage survey – Health Facility module (Global Fund)*		EUV*	EUV* Health Facility Survey (to be conducted)	EUV	EUV	EUV	EUV
Malaria surveillance and routine system support						Revised malaria indicators in HMIS	Health facility-based longitudinal data collection (proposed)		
Other data sources					Studies conducted by Maferinyah Training & Research Center: • TES • 3-arm clinical trial (AS-pyronaridine, AS-piperaquine, AS-AQ) • Malaria study including biomarkers, entomology data, and knowledge, attitudes, and practices				

* Report available

38

Progress during the last 12 months

M&E activities have shown varying degrees of progress in the last year due to the delayed award of the malaria bilateral. Despite this delay, several important M&E activities have taken place.

Routine data and HMIS strengthening: The *Bureau de Statistiques et de Développement* and the NMCP have worked, with the support of a PMI implementing partner, to revise the HMIS form for malaria to capture key epidemiological and stock management data on one form. The new form includes the following indicators: number of suspect malaria cases, cases tested (microscopy and RDT), cases confirmed positive (microscopy and RDT), cases treated with ACT, severe cases treated with ACT, cases referred, and deceased. Numbers are reported for the health facility, as well as by community health agents. Data are also included from ANC including total women seen in ANC, number receiving first dose of SP, number receiving at least three doses of SP, and number of women sensitized at ANC. Cascade training on completing this new form has just begun.

2012 DHS: The 2012 DHS was implemented from June-October 2012, and a preliminary report has been disseminated. This survey provides the first nationally representative estimates of malaria parasitemia. Because it was implemented in the rainy season, these estimates will be comparable to the MIS, which will be implemented in the summer of 2014. Additionally, the DHS provides important baseline measures for ITN coverage and use because it was implemented prior to the 2013 mass ITN distribution campaign. The MIS, which will be conducted 9-12 months after the campaign, will provide important post-campaign coverage estimates.

EUV Survey: Two EUV surveys were conducted in the last year. One, conducted in December 2012, found relatively high levels of ACT stockouts in the previous 3 months (50-100% of facilities sampled), but showed better results for ACT stocks on the day of the survey due to a recent PMI emergency procurement and distribution. Additional results showed that only 36% of staff was trained in case management. Roughly half of all malaria cases were diagnosed based on clinical symptoms alone and one-third of these cases did not receive an appropriate antimalarial. The second survey, conducted in April 2013, showed better results for ACT stocks due to additional PMI distributions. However, RDTs were still not widely available in facilities, resulting in clinical diagnosis for cases. Increased donor procurement of RDTs, continued procurement of ACTs, and NMCP revisions to treatment guidelines and training materials will hopefully mitigate this situation.

Therapeutic efficacy studies: Researchers at the Maferinyah Research and Training Center are conducting ongoing therapeutic efficacy studies for Guinea's first-line ACT, AS-AQ. The studies follow the WHO protocol, and are funded by the European & Developing Countries Clinical Trials Partnership. Data collection is still ongoing, but preliminary results show 94% efficacy for AS-AQ. The Maferinyah Research and Training Center is also conducting a three-arm clinical trial of artesunate-pyronaridine, artesunate-piperaquine, and AS-AQ. The Maferinyah researchers have also begun a study aimed at examining the seasonal burden of malaria (in low transmission and high transmission seasons) in the four different climatic zones (low-lying, middle, high, and forested). The data collection will also include entomological parameters, as well as individuals' knowledge, attitudes, and practices related to malaria prevention and treatment.

Challenges, opportunities & threats

One primary challenge is related to the capacity of the NMCP to coordinate and realize its national M&E strategy. The M&E strategic plan for 2013-2017 has yet to be finalized, and this should serve as the road map for all partners' M&E activities, including PMI. Also, substantial constraints with respect to infrastructure and equipment exist at the NMCP. The M&E unit in the NMCP is relatively young, but enthusiastic and quite aware of the objectives that need to be accomplished. With the momentum behind the awarding of PMI's new bilateral, the potential is high for realizing the foundational elements required for building M&E capacity at the NMCP.

An additional M&E challenge is related to the manner in which the country is "divided" between PMI and Global Fund target zones. While this division has worked well for distribution of commodities, it poses a greater challenge for tasks that need to be coordinated at a central level and implemented on a national scale, such as training, supervision, and most M&E activities (e.g., national surveys, evaluation of LLIN mass campaign, HMIS revision, and routine system strengthening). Addressing this challenge requires strong NMCP leadership and communication to ensure they are guiding and directing key decisions. From the very beginning of PMI's work in Guinea, the country team noted the need to strengthen the NMCP's coordination role, and progress appears to have been made in this area. The new bilateral will continue to support and address this need, and the country team will monitor whether or not national-level interventions are being implemented in a coordinated fashion and will communicate with our Global Fund colleagues as needed.

In addition to building on positive momentum with the NMCP and the new bilateral, an additional opportunity for strengthening malaria M&E in Guinea and building a knowledge base to inform programming and interventions is the research being conducted at the Maferinyah Training and Research Center. The center's research director is engaged in several multi-site studies, including clinical trials, therapeutic efficacy studies, parasitemia surveys, and entomological monitoring. The relationship between the NMCP and research center currently appears to be tenuous with minimal collaboration. The in-country PMI team, particularly with the arrival of the new CDC Resident Advisor, will work to strengthen this collaboration and ensure the data generated are made accessible to the NMCP and other malaria partners in Guinea.

Plans and justification

In its fourth year of implementation, PMI will continue to build on gains made in strengthening Guinea's M&E system for malaria. With the 2012 DHS and 2014 MIS, key malaria baseline indicators for intervention coverage and impact (including parasitemia) are available. PMI will consider funding needed for the 2017 DHS in the FY 2015 MOP. A health facility survey will provide nationally representative baseline data for facility readiness to provide needed malaria services and case management practices once training and commodities for case management are rolled out on a national scale. PMI will continue data collection on commodity availability through the EUV survey to provide rapidly available and actionable data.

To complement the commodity data collected through EUV surveys and case management data collected through the health facility survey, a health facility-based surveillance system will provide longitudinal data to better monitor trends in malaria burden at a selection of health facilities. The data generated by this system will ensure high data quality at select sites and an opportunity to better understand epidemiological trends in Guinea. The country team, with technical assistance from the PMI M&E team, will work with the implementing partner to ensure an appropriate surveillance model is implemented for the Guinea country context. Additional details on the proposed surveillance model are available in a separate activity proposal. While quality-controlled data are collected at select surveillance sites, PMI will continue to capitalize on gains made in HMIS strengthening. Assuming training on reporting and data quality have been carried out on a national level, routine system strengthening activities will put a greater focus on data use. Activities undertaken will have measureable objectives, and will include developing and disseminating specific data use products, such as a national malaria bulletin. Additional details on the proposed activities for routine system strengthening are available in a separate activity proposal. Though no funds are budgeted for operational research projects, the Guinea team will work to technically support ongoing and new operational research projects in the country and ensure strong links between the NMCP and researchers.

Proposed activities with FY 2014 funding: ($562,500)

1. *EUV survey:* The EUV survey will continue to be implemented to monitor the availability and use of key malaria control commodities at the health facility level. These surveys will be expanded beyond the PMI target zones to provide rapid results to inform logistics management for key commodities on a national scale. Improved logistics management is directly related to the health system's ability to provide effective case management for malaria *($150,000)*;

2. *Health facility-based surveillance:* A surveillance system will provide longitudinal data on seasonal trends in malaria cases at a selection of health facilities. The system will have clear and simple objectives and indicators, with sites selected based on explicit criteria. To the extent possible, sites will be selected from previously functioning sentinel sites *($200,000)*;

3. *Routine system strengthening*: Routine system strengthening activities will continue to build upon progress made in M&E training at the district, regional, and national levels. Activities will focus on ensuring data quality (including completeness, timeliness, and accuracy) while maximizing data use for decision-making. Specific activities with measurable objectives will be identified based on ongoing assessments of progress and gaps *($200,000)*; and

4. *Technical assistance for M&E:* A CDC M&E temporary duty visit will provide technical assistance for ongoing M&E activities including health facility-based surveillance and routine system strengthening. The country team and USAID mission will help define the priority objectives for this TDY *($12,500)*.

Behavior Change Communication

NMCP/PMI objectives

In the updated draft national strategy (2013-2017), the NMCP highlights the important role of BCC across interventions by specifying an objective related to adoption of target behaviors for malaria control and prevention. The first target for the objective is to develop and disseminate a coordinated communication plan for all relevant partners and stakeholders in Guinea. The strategy also highlights the important role of a partnership to coordinate BCC messages, tools, and processes, including pre-testing, validation, and distribution of support materials.

The NMCP developed a communication plan in 2009, which was revised with PMI support in March 2012 (to cover the period 2012-2015). The new communication plan emphasizes comprehensive communication activities based on formative research, including interpersonal and mass media approaches, adequately supported through training and educational materials and appropriately monitored and evaluated. It also identifies key behaviors and describes challenges, barriers, and opportunities for adoption of those behaviors. The new PMI bilateral project will be responsible for BCC activities for LLIN use, IPTp, and community case management in the PMI target zones. In addition to PMI, the Global Fund is also providing support for BCC activities related to case management and the LLIN mass campaign. Because multiple partners– including PMI, Global Fund, and each donor's implementers – are responsible for BCC activities for malaria across the country, a coordinated plan is essential to ensure consistent messaging and complementary approaches to carrying out the plan.

Progress during the last 12 months

PMI progress on BCC in the last year has included revision of the NMCP's national communication plan and training manual used by animators for BCC techniques related to malaria prevention and treatment. In addition, 219 health workers in the PMI target zones were trained on malaria case management, including a BCC component. A similar training was conducted for 206 CHWs. In addition to case management supplies, CHWs were given job aid posters and story boards to ensure they had proper information to do their job and to conduct sensitization sessions on malaria prevention and treatment for their community members. Partner activities also included training 23 NGO animators on BCC related to malaria prevention, and supporting 2 Peace Corps Volunteers to work with local NGOs on implementing malaria BCC activities in the region of Boke and Conakry. The revised national communication plan, training materials, and tools are used not only in the PMI target areas, but also by the Global Fund implementers in the remaining areas of the country.

Activities for BCC have primarily focused on increasing ANC attendance and IPTp 2 uptake, as well as increasing early care seeking for fever. These PMI activities were part of an integrated mechanism for family and child health in targeted the PMI zones (14 prefectures and five communes of Conakry). The BCC activities included both interpersonal communication through peer discussion groups, as well as mass media through radio, television, and pamphlet distribution. Radio and televisions spots were translated and broadcast in four local languages. Three pamphlets were developed and distributed which include general information on malaria, as well as specific information on IPTp and bed net use. Key messages were developed in a participatory manner based on the national malaria communication plan and were pre-tested during focus groups with literate and non-literate community members. Target audiences were pregnant women, mothers, and health care providers.

The PMI BCC implementing partner had a relatively short timeframe in which to carry out its activities, and no evaluation was conducted to assess outcomes or impact of the activities. The partner reported reaching an estimated 169,000 members of the target audience through interpersonal communications. No data are available for reach of mass media channels and the implementing partner acknowledges that this is a significant challenge for conducting M&E of BCC.

In the immediate future, the new PMI bilateral project will focus BCC activities on the mass LLIN universal coverage campaign to sensitize communities to the distribution as well as proper use and care of nets, including hang-up. Careful review of the partner work plan will ensure all planned BCC activities are carried out in the next year to complement the NMCP national communication plan.

Challenges, opportunities & threats

New national policies related to IPTp, use of diagnostics for case confirmation, and scale up of community case management require updated BCC messaging and tools to ensure information and training are coordinated and consistent with national policies. Because multiple partners are implementing BCC activities across the country, clear documentation of the plans and policies are essential. The finalization of these key documents has had some delays, but these essential tasks are built into partner work plans.

M&E of BCC is a challenge, not only in Guinea, but in other PMI countries as well. Approaches and methodologies for conducting effective BCC M&E have yet to be standardized, and many BCC implementing partners simply do not have the capacity to conduct the more rigorous evaluation designs required for linking interventions to behavioral outcomes. The global malaria community is continuing to work on guidance for BCC indicators and evaluation. Guinea may provide a suitable environment for piloting novel approaches to conducting simple evaluation of BCC interventions.

The integration of BCC training and tools into health worker and CHW case management training has been an efficient and strategic means to ensure that community members not only receive proper malaria care, but are also provided with the information needed to protect themselves from contracting malaria and to prevent development of severe infection.

Plans and justification

PMI will continue to support the NMCP's communication plan with implementation of BCC activities in the PMI target zones reflecting NMCP priorities and national policies, including ITN use, ANC attendance and IPTp uptake, and case management, including RDT and ACT use. Proposed activities will consist of a mix of interpersonal communication approaches and mass media and will be developed based on formative research and pre-testing using participatory approaches to ensure they are culturally appropriate and resonate with the target audience. Future

BCC interventions will have an increased focus on M&E to measure outputs, outcomes, and impact of activities.

Proposed activities with FY 2014 funding

1. *BCC for ITNs, IPTp, and case management:* BCC will be part of an integrated communication package including ITN use, IPTp uptake, and case management at the health facility and community levels. Activities will be focused in the PMI target zones but will be consistent with the NMCP's national communication plan and national policies, and coordinated with BCC activities in the rest of the country *($600,000).*

Health System Strengthening and Capacity Building

PMI/NMCP objectives

The MOH has assigned several objectives to the NMCP, the most important of which are to:
- Promote the national malaria control policy based on the RBM partnership principles;
- Formulate and facilitate the approval of the national malaria strategic plan to reduce morbidity and mortality due to malaria;
- Elaborate, monitor, and evaluate implementation of the national malaria strategic plan on an annual basis;
- Mobilize and manage human, financial and material resources necessary for the implementation of the national malaria strategic plan; and
- Promote and develop partnerships with all stakeholders in the control of malaria.

The new National Malaria Strategic Plan (2013-2017), yet to be validated, calls for the strengthening of the management capacity of the NMCP in order to achieve the above listed objectives of the program. This includes assigning an appropriate number of staff to the program that have the technical as well as managerial and leadership capacity to effectively coordinate the program.

Situation analysis
The Guinea NMCP is staffed with a dozen professionals led by a Coordinator and a Deputy Coordinator and comprises five entomologists (the five entomologists are biologists who act as entomologists), three M&E specialists, four biologists, and one accountant. Most of the staff members have been working at the NMCP during the past five years and thus have good knowledge of the program. Recently, the NMCP has been reshuffled by the Minister of Health, bringing new staff on board. Although MOH officials state that the GOG supports the salary of the majority of the program personnel, no information is available on the GOG's budgetary contribution to program operations. The NMCP receives financial support from the Global Fund to cover many operating expenses, including salary for part of the staff, office supplies, transportation means, and gas for routine operations.

Overall, the Guinea health system suffers from a lack of qualified health workers at all levels. In an attempt to fill this gap, in 2011the GOG recruited 1,300 health workers, including physicians, nurses, midwives, and laboratory technicians who were deployed throughout the country. In addition, the GOG plans to increase the number of CHWs to provide health care services, mainly malaria prevention and community case management, to the 60% of the population who do not use public health facilities. The GOG plans to strengthen the capacity of approximately 3,000 CHWs to provide better quality of community case management. The current gap in human resources (in all categories) in the health system is estimated at 3,000, for which funding has yet to be identified.

Efforts are underway at the MOH to integrate health interventions to improve the performance of the health system. During the last six years, a lack of supervision has affected the quality of malaria case management. Support for training provided by malaria donors has also suffered from lack of coordination by the NMCP, which has contributed to the poor performance of the health system.

Progress during the last 12 months

Health System Strengthening
In FY 2013, PMI supported a wide range of health system strengthening activities, including:
- Support to the NMCP to establish a national committee for malaria control that holds monthly meetings using the RBM coordination model;
- Mapping of malaria interventions and partners in Guinea;
- Monthly monitoring visits to the district level;
- Support of the review of the national malaria strategic plan and development of the new strategy (2013-2017);
- Support to the NMCP to develop and harmonize data collection and supervision tools at both health facilities and community levels; and
- Support to the national directorate of prevention to develop and validate the national community health policy.

PMI also supported the following capacity building activities:
- Strengthening capacity of local NGOs to participate in malaria prevention activities;
- Training of 419 health workers on malaria control (prevention, RDTs, treatment, and interpersonal communication) in 11 Prefectures in the PMI-supported areas
- Training of 206 CHWs on malaria community case management of uncomplicated malaria, referral of severe malaria and BCC
- Support to the NMCP to train supervisors at the central, regional, and district levels.

In addition, PMI supported activities to strengthen the partnership between the NMCP and civil society's organizations. This includes training 23 NGO animators on BCC related to malaria prevention and distribution of 12,000 bed nets in the 17 villages of the rural commune of Kouankan in Macenta and 11 villages of Maferinyah. Also, two Peace Corps Volunteers worked with local NGOs on implementing malaria BCC activities in the region of Boke and Conakry.

Challenges, opportunities, and threats

Lack of governance is a common plague in Guinea with rampant corruption, making operations in the health system more costly and access to health care more difficult for communities with limited resources. The current transition from a military regime to a multi-party democracy provides a window of opportunity for the advancement of good governance, transparency, and professionalization within the public health care system. However, the country has yet to pay enough attention to improving or enforcing rules and regulations pertaining to public services.

A lack of accountability among health providers is weakening the system's commitment to service provision to care seekers. Inadequate distribution of qualified health care providers throughout the country is a key barrier to delivery of services. The health sector continues to suffer from lack of skilled providers, particularly in the interior of the country. Hiring practices are non-transparent and staff hiring is barely based on skills needed and competencies. At the lower level of the health system, mainly at service delivery points, in 2011 the GOG has endeavored to recruit and assign almost 1,300 health workers throughout the country, but that number is far below the important personnel gaps in the country to meet service delivery requirements. To fill the gap of services at the community level, given the low health facility use rate, donors such as PMI have supported the design of a community health strategy that has recently been disseminated, with the expectation that the MOH will validate and adopt it in the near future for implementation. However, the issue of motivating CHWs remains a real challenge.

Guinea possesses several training institutions that can work with the NMCP to provide on-the job training as well as refresher training. One of them is the National Institute for Public Health, which has developed malaria training modules and conducted research activities, the most recent of which is a pilot study on malaria case management in health facilities. In addition, the National Nursing School of Kindia trains hundreds of nurses in a three-year program. The Maferinyah Training and Research Center supported by the African Development Bank and the European & Developing Countries Clinical Trials Partnership represents an opportunity for health system strengthening as it is staffed by highly qualified experts who were trained at the Malaria Research and Training Center in Mali.

The new national malaria strategic plan was designed with support from RBM, PMI and other partners. In preparation for the evaluation of the strategic plan, the NMCP has identified several key capacity building priorities:
- Organization of quarterly meetings to review and validate malaria data and information;
- Supervision at the regional and prefectural levels;
- Support to quarterly supervision by the central level of the MOH; and
- Strengthening the capacity of CHWs.

A large part of the NMCP operations cost is paid by the Global Fund, and with the uncertainty of the disbursement of the consolidated Round 6 and 10 grants (for various reasons), the NMCP needs a strong managerial capacity to meet the disbursement requirements and avoid unnecessary delays or suspension of Global Fund activities.

Plans and justification

Given the challenges facing malaria prevention and control in Guinea, PMI resources will be used to address priorities that are directly linked to malaria service delivery. PMI will work with other donors to improve coordination to enable the NMCP to progressively fill service delivery gaps. Moreover, PMI plans to conduct an assessment of NMCP organizational capacity to identify and address weaknesses. PMI also plans to recruit a senior-level manager to work closely with the NMCP to facilitate smooth implementation and M&E of Global Fund activities, and enable timely disbursement of planned Global Fund resources. Such a position will be funded outside of the PMI budget.

With FY 2014 funding, in addition to supporting training and supervision of health workers and CHWs in effective malaria case management, PMI plans to put a special emphasis on strengthening the capacity of the NMCP, based on the recommendations of the organizational assessment. Because the award of the implementing mechanism has been significantly delayed, funding in the bilateral pipeline will be used to complement the resources programmed under this section and cover activities planned for FY 2014. The capacity gaps will be identified in technical areas such as case management, entomology, M&E, and BCC; training will be provided to staff members at each level of the health system. Other capacity building activities include supporting entomological training and formalizing a partnership between the NMCP and Peace Corps.

Proposed activities with FY 2014 funding: ($150,000)

1. *Training of NMCP personnel* in Guinea based on clearly identified capacity building needs in areas such as M&E, case management, diagnostics, surveillance, or BCC. The NMCP will be asked to prioritize and justify training needs *($30,000)*;

2. *Support to the NMCP* to assist them in team building, logistics and supervision, office management including communication capacity/connectivity, and M&E systems strengthening *($100,000)*; and

3. *Support to Peace Corps*: Maintain a Response Volunteer in Conakry and support to supervise volunteers who are supporting PMI activities *($20,000)*.

Staffing & Administration

Two health professionals serve as Resident Advisors to oversee the PMI in Guinea, one representing CDC and one representing USAID. In addition, one or more Foreign Service Nationals work as part of the PMI team. All PMI staff members are part of a single inter-agency team led by the USAID Mission Director or his/her designee in country. The PMI team shares responsibility for development and implementation of PMI strategies and work plans, coordination with national authorities, managing collaborating agencies and supervising day-to-day activities. Candidates for resident advisor positions (whether initial hires or replacements) will be evaluated and/or interviewed jointly by USAID and CDC, and both agencies will be involved in hiring decisions, with the final decision made by the individual agency.

The PMI professional staff work together to oversee all technical and administrative aspects of the PMI, including finalizing details of the project design, implementing malaria prevention and treatment activities, monitoring and evaluation of outcomes and impact, reporting of results, and providing guidance to PMI partners.

The PMI lead in country is the USAID Mission Director. The two PMI resident advisors, one from USAID and one from CDC, report to the Senior USAID Health Officer for day-to-day leadership, and work together as a part of a single interagency team. The technical expertise housed in Atlanta and Washington guides PMI programmatic efforts and thus overall technical guidance for both RAs falls to the PMI staff in Atlanta and Washington. Since CDC resident advisors are CDC employees (CDC USDD—38), responsibility for completing official performance reviews lies with the CDC Country Director who is expected to rely upon input from PMI staff across the two agencies that work closely day in and day out with the CDC RA and thus best positioned to comment on the RA's performance.

The two PMI resident advisors are based within the USAID health office and are expected to spend approximately half their time sitting with and providing technical assistance to the national malaria control programs and partners.

Locally-hired staff to support PMI activities either in Ministries or in USAID will be approved by the USAID Mission Director. Because of the need to adhere to specific country policies and USAID accounting regulations, any transfer of PMI funds directly to Ministries or host governments will need to be approved by the USAID Mission Director and Controller, in addition to the PMI Coordinator.

Proposed activities with FY 2014 funding: ($1,100,000)

1. *USAID technical staff:* Support one Resident Advisor and one foreign service national to support malaria activities and administration costs*($700,000)*; and

2. *CDC technical staff:* Support one Resident Advisor to support malaria activities and administration costs *($400,000)*.

TABLE 1

President's Malaria Initiative – *Guinea*
FY 2014 Budget Breakdown by Partner ($10,000,000)

Partner Organization	Geographic Area	Activity	Budget
USAID/Deliver Project	PMI Target Areas and Nationwide	Procure LLINs, SP, RDTs, microscopes, and Injectable Artesunate	5,130,000
Stop Palu	PMI Target Areas and Nationwide	Entomological monitoring, LLIN distribution, BCC, training, supervision, diagnostics, capacity building, EUV survey, strengthening HMIS	2,912,000
Systems for Improved Access to Pharmaceuticals and Services	National Level	Capacity development in logistics management, pharmaceutical systems reform, and improving drug regulatory capacity	800,000
Peace Corps	Nationwide	Support Response Volunteers	20,000
CDC Interagency Agreement	National	Technical Assistance for Entomology, Community Case Management, and M&E	37,500
	Conakry	One Resident Advisor	400,000
USAID/Guinea	Conakry	One Resident Advisor and One Locally-engaged Staff	700,000
		TOTAL	**10,000,000**

TABLE 2
President's Malaria Initiative – *Guinea*
Planned Obligations for FY 2014 ($10,000,000)

Proposed Activity	Mechanism	Budget	Geographic Area	Description of Activity
PREVENTION				
Insecticide-Treated Nets				
1. Procurement and delivery of LLINs	USAID/Deliver Project	610,000	PMI Target Areas	Procure and deliver to the district level 180,000 LLINs to be distributed for routine ANC services for pregnant women. This will contribute to covering approximately 73% of routine distribution needs for pregnant women.
2. Distribution of routine LLINs	Stop Palu	180,000	PMI Target Areas	Pay for distribution costs of routine nets from the district level to health facilities.
3. BCC for LLIN use	Stop Palu	Cost covered under BCC section	PMI Target Areas	BCC for ITN use will be part of an integrated communication package including MIP and case management, following national standards and in conjunction with what other donors are doing in their respective target areas.
	Subtotal: ITNs	**$790,000**		
Indoor Residual Spraying				
1. Entomological monitoring and capacity building	Stop Palu	150,000	Nationwide	Entomological monitoring and surveillance of vectors for insecticide resistance, and capacity building for entomologists and insectary development and management.
2. Technical assistance for entomological capacity building	CDC IAA	25,000	Nationwide	Funding for two technical assistance visits from CDC to help develop entomological capacity at the national and prefectural level.

Proposed Activity	Mechanism	Budget	Geographic Area	Description of Activity
Malaria in Pregnancy	**Subtotal: IRS**	**$175,000**		
1. Procure treatments of SP	USAID/Deliver Project	57,500	Nationwide	Procure approximately 1,437,500 treatments of SP to contribute to covering nationwide needs (490,000 estimated potential pregnancies receiving 3 doses of SP during pregnancy).
2. Supplies to ensure consumption of SP at ANC	Stop Palu	5,000	Nationwide	Supplies such as cups and water to ensure that SP is taken at the time of ANC visit.
3. BCC for IPTp	Stop Palu	Cost covered under BCC section	Nationwide	Support BCC to promote ANC clinic attendance and educate pregnant women and communities on the benefits of IPTp. This activity will include support for community-level approaches, such as training of community-based workers as well as mass media (including local radio stations). Immunization outreach sessions will be used as opportunities for educating women. This will be part of a larger integrated BCC activity to satisfy needs for case management, LLINs, and IPTp.
4. Training/Refresher training for	Stop Palu	Cost covered under Case Management/Diagnostics section	PMI Target Areas	Provide training and refresher training for public and private health facility midwives and nurses to correctly deliver SP in the context of the focused antenatal care approach. Training will include benchmark assessments, on-the-job training of the new treatment algorithm, and coaching. Training will be part of an integrated training package.
5. Supervise health workers in IPTp to improve quality of service	Stop Palu	Cost covered under Case Management/Diagnostics section	PMI Target Areas	On-site supervision for public health facility midwives and nurses to correctly deliver SP in the context of the focused antenatal care approach. Supervision will continue to be part of an integrated approach for supervision at health facilities.

Proposed Activity	Mechanism	Budget	Geographic Area	Description of Activity
Subtotal: Malaria in Pregnancy		**$62,500**		
CASE MANAGEMENT				
Diagnosis				
1. Procure rapid diagnostics tests (RDTs)	USAID/Deliver Project	2,800,000	PMI Target Areas	Procure approximately 4,515,000 RDTs to continue scaling up RDT use in health facilities and in communities via CHWs.
2. Procure microscopes and consumables	USAID/Deliver Project	50,000	PMI Target Areas	Procure 15 microscopes, reagents, slides and repair materials for hospitals as well as reagents, slides and repair materials for previously purchased microscopes.
3. Improved malaria diagnostics	Stop Palu	200,000	Nationwide	Work with the NMCP and National Laboratory to develop and support a comprehensive quality assurance and quality control plan for malaria diagnostics at all levels of the health system. This will include refresher training for lab technicians (and training on malaria microscopy for new laboratory technicians) and regular supervision of microscopy and RDT performance, including systematic review of a predetermined number of positive and negative blood smears and simultaneous use of both tests to assess the quality of RDTs in diagnosing malaria.
4. Training/refresher training in RDT use	Stop Palu	600,000	PMI Target Areas	Refresher training on malaria diagnostics, including correct RDT use at all levels of the health care system. New health care workers and CHWs will be trained with FY 2013 funding. (This will be an integrated RDT/case management training. See Case Management section for detailed description of case management training component.)

Proposed Activity	Mechanism	Budget	Geographic Area	Description of Activity
5. Supervision of health workers and CHWs in RDT use	Stop Palu	360,000	PMI Target Areas	Integrated, regular supervision of health workers and CHWs focusing on microscopy and RDT performance. (This will be integrated RDT/case management supervision. See Case Management section for detailed description of case management supervision component.)
Subtotal: Diagnosis		**$4,010,000**		
Treatment				
1. Procure and distribute ACTs	USAID/Deliver Project	990,000	PMI Target Areas	Procure and distribute approximately 1,833,000 ACTs.
2.Procurement of injectable artesunate	USAID/Deliver Project	180,000	PMI Target Areas	PMI will fund procurement of approximately 71,300 treatments of injectable artesunate for severe malaria.
3.BCC for case management	Stop Palu	Cost covered under BCC section	PMI Target Areas	FY 2014 funds will be used to fund integrated behavior change communication and education activities for communities to improve behaviors related to malaria prevention and treatment. The BCC supported in 2014 will target prevention activities, including use of LLINs and IPTp. BCC activities will also support appropriate care seeking behaviors, particularly at the community level through use of CHWs. Particular emphasis will be placed on prompt care-seeking for fever and other symptoms of malaria.
4. Clinical training/refresher training in malaria case management	Stop Palu	Cost covered under Case Management/Diagnostics section	PMI Target Areas	Training in RDT use, malaria case management, and malaria in pregnancy for health workers at hospitals, health centers, and health posts who have not been trained using previous years funds.Also, M&E training for district and regional level

Proposed Activity	Mechanism	Budget	Geographic Area	Description of Activity
				officials. Training of CHWs not yet trained in RDT use, in treatment of uncomplicated malaria and referral for patients with severe malaria, as well as referral of pregnant women to ANCs. Continue implementation of a comprehensive refresher training schedule for health workers and CHWs who have already received initial training.
5. Supervision of health workers and CHWs	Stop Palu	Cost covered under Case Management/Diagnostics section	PMI Target Areas	Enhance clinical supervision at all levels of the health care system, including hospitals, health centers, health posts, and CHWs. District Health Team staff (*Département Préfectoral de Santé*) and regional health team staff (*Département Régional de Santé*) will be actively involved in supervision activities, along with health center staff for supervision of CHWs. Supervision visits will include observation of patient consultations and feedback to providers.
6. Community case management	Stop Palu	130,000	PMI Target Areas	Support the scale-up of community case management in PMI target areas, including management and logistic costs, and support for data management, as well as training of 650 CHWs.
Subtotal: Treatment		**$1,300,000**		
Pharmaceutical Management				
1. Logistic management information systems	Systems for Improved Access to Pharmaceuticals and Services	100,000	National and Regional Level	Continued support to strengthen the Logistics Management Information System to enable the pharmaceutical system collect, compile and process consumption data throughout the health system in order to improve the forecasting, the procurement and the distribution of commodities. Includes

Proposed Activity	Mechanism	Budget	Geographic Area	Description of Activity
				procurement of computers, support for Internet connectivity, capacity building for quantification at the central level (PCG, DNPL) as well as at the regional, prefectures and district levels.
2. Pharmaceutical systems reform	Systems for Improved Access to Pharmaceuticals and Services	250,000	National Level	Continue to support the reform of regulations governing the supply chain management system, including advocacy for signing a convention between the Government and PCG and improvement of the governance of PCG (renewal and functioning of the board, information sharing, civil society and private sector's participation, etc.).
3.Improve drug regulatory capacity	Systems for Improved Access to Pharmaceuticals and Services	300,000	National Level	Continue to support improvement of the regulatory and oversight capacities of the DNPL, revision of national list of essential drugs and enhanced control of compliance to the pharmaceutical policy and regulations by PCG and the private pharmacies network.
4. Management of pharmaceutical supplies	USAID/Deliver Project	600,000	National Level	Manage the distribution of PMI commodities down to the health facility level, including warehousing, transportation, storage and distribution.
Subtotal: Pharmaceutical Management		**$1,250,000**		
MONITORING AND EVALUATION/OPERATIONS RESEARCH				
1. End-use Verification	Systems for Improved Access to Pharmaceuticals and Services	150,000	Nationwide	Provide support to monitor the availability and utilization of key antimalarial commodities at the health facility level.
2. Health facility-based surveillance	Stop Palu	200,000	Nationwide	Revitalization of previously functioning sentinel sites (under previous Global Fund grants) in order

55

Proposed Activity	Mechanism	Budget	Geographic Area	Description of Activity
				to provide longitudinal data on trends in malaria cases throughout the country.
3. Routine system strengthening	Stop Palu	200,000	Nationwide	Implement activities to strengthen routine malaria data quality (including completeness, timeliness, and accuracy) and data use for decision making. Activities will be prioritized based on identified gaps and weaknesses.
4. Technical assistance for M&E	CDC IAA	12,500	Nationwide	Technical support to the NMCP for ongoing M&E activities including routine system strengthening and NMCP M&E capacity building.
Subtotal: M&E		**$562,500**		
BEHAVIOUR CHANGE COMMUNICATION				
1. BCC for ITN and IPT use as well as for use of case management (RDT and ACT use)	Stop Palu	600,000	PMI Target Areas	BCC will be part of integrated communication package including ITN use and MIP and will include case management at both the facility and community levels, following national standards and in conjunction with what other donors are doing in their respective target areas. This activity will be implemented in health districts targeted by PMI, using the NMCP communication plan.
Subtotal: BCC		**$600,000**		
HEALTH SYSTEMS STRENGTHENING/CAPACITY BUILDING				
1. Training of NMCP staff	Stop Palu	30,000	National and Prefectural Levels	Training of NMCP personnel in Guinea based on clearly identified capacity building needs in areas such as M&E, case management, diagnostics, surveillance, or BCC. The NMCP will be asked to prioritize and justify training needs.

Proposed Activity	Mechanism	Budget	Geographic Area	Description of Activity
2. Management support for NMCP	Stop Palu	100,000	National and Prefectural Levels	Support to the NMCP to assist them in team building, logistics and supervision, office management including communication capacity/connectivity, and M&E systems strengthening.
3. Peace Corps Response Volunteer	Peace Corps/SPA	20,000	NA	Support to maintain two Response Volunteers in Conakry and to supervise volunteers throughout the country.
Subtotal: Capacity Building		**$150,000**		
STAFFING AND ADMINISTRATION				
1. USAID Resident Advisor and Locally Engaged Senior Malaria Advisor	USAID	700,000	Conakry	Support for one USAID PMI Advisor and one USAID locally-engaged senior malaria specialist as well as one CDC PMI Advisor, and all related local costs to sitting in USAID Mission.
2. CDC Resident Advisor	CDC IAA	400,000	Conakry	
Subtotal: In-country Management and Administration		**$1,100,000**		
GRAND TOTAL		**$10,000,000**